Fix It!™ Grammar

Frog Prince
STUDENT BOOK
LEVEL 5

Pamela White

Fourth Edition, January 2022
Institute for Excellence in Writing, L.L.C.

Copyright Policy

Fix It! Grammar: Frog Prince, Student Book Level 5
Fourth Edition, January 2022
Second Printing version 3, April 2022
Copyright © 2022 Institute for Excellence in Writing

ISBN 978-1-62341-365-1

Our duplicating/copying policy for *Fix It! Grammar: Frog Prince*, Student Book Level 5:

All rights reserved.

No part of this book may be reproduced, stored in a retrieval system, or transmitted in any form or by any means, electronic, mechanical, photocopying, recording, or otherwise, without the prior written permission of the publisher, except as provided by U.S.A. copyright law and the specific policy below:

Home use: The purchaser may copy this Student Book for use by multiple children within his or her immediate family. Each family must purchase its own Student Book.

Small group or co-op classes: Each participating student or family is required to purchase a Student Book. A teacher may not copy from this Student Book.

Classroom teachers: A Student Book must be purchased for each participating student. A teacher may not copy from this Student Book.

Additional copies of this Student Book may be purchased from IEW.com/FIX-L5-S

Institute for Excellence in Writing (IEW®)
8799 N. 387 Road
Locust Grove, OK 74352
800.856.5815
info@IEW.com
IEW.com

Printed in Illinois, United States of America

IEW® and Structure and Style® are registered trademarks of the Institute for Excellence in Writing, L.L.C.

Fix It!™ is a trademark of the Institute for Excellence in Writing, L.L.C.

Instructions

The list below shows the components to each *Fix It! Grammar* weekly exercise.

Although in Levels 1–4 students could choose to either Mark It or Fix It first, in Levels 5 and 6, students must complete the passages in this order: **Read It**, **Mark It**, **Fix It**. After Week 4 students should number the sentence openers after the passage has been marked and fixed.

Students should discuss their work with the teacher after working through each daily passage. However, older students may work with their teacher on a weekly basis. Students should actively be involved in comparing their work with the Teacher's Manual. The repetition of finding and fixing their own mistakes allows them to recognize and avoid those mistakes in the future.

Fix It! Grammar should be treated as a game. Keep it fun!

Learn It! On the first day of the new Week, read through the Learn It section. Each Learn It covers a concept that the student will practice in future passages. Instructions for marking and fixing passages are included in each Learn It.

Read It! Read the day's passage.
Look up the bolded vocabulary word in a dictionary and pick the definition that fits the context of the story. Maintain a list of vocabulary words and their definitions.
The vocabulary definitions are printed in the Teacher's Manual.

Mark It! Mark the passage using the guide at the top of the daily practice page.

Fix It! Correct the passage using the guide at the top of the daily practice page.
The Teacher's Manual includes detailed explanations for grammar concepts and punctuation in each daily passage.

Rewrite It! After marking, correcting, and discussing the passage with the teacher, copy the corrected passage on the lines provided or into a separate notebook.
- Copy the corrected story, not the editing marks.
- Indent and use capital letters properly.
- Copy the corrected punctuation.

Editing Marks

¶ indent
∧ insert
⌒ delete
= capitalize
/ lowercase
⌒ reverse order
add a space
⌒ close the space

Helpful Hints
Use different colors for **Mark It** and **Fix It**.

Appendix I Complete Story Familiarize yourself with the story that you will be editing by reading the complete story found in Appendix I.

Appendix II Collection Pages Look for strong verbs, quality adjectives, and -ly adverbs in this book and write them on the collection pages in Appendix II.

Appendix III Lists Refer to the lists found in Appendix III to quickly identify pronouns, prepositions, verbs, conjunctions, clauses, phrases, and sentence openers.

Appendix IV Grammar Glossary Reference the Grammar Glossary found in Appendix IV of the Teacher's Manual for more information about the concepts taught in the *Fix It! Grammar* series.

Additional Resource

Fix It! Grammar Cards are an optional product that will enhance the *Fix It! Grammar* learning experience.

Fix It! Grammar Cards

Thirty full color grammar cards highlight key *Fix It! Grammar* concepts for quick and easy reference.

For a more relaxed and entertaining way to drill and review grammar concepts learned, instructions for a download of multiple game ideas are included in the card pack.

Fix It! Grammar Cards are beautifully designed and come in a sturdy card box for easy storage.

IEW.com/FIX-GC

On the chart below *Fix It! Grammar Cards* are listed in the order that the information is taught in this book.

WEEK	Fix It! Grammar Cards for *Frog Prince* Level 5
1	Editing Marks, Capitalization, Indentation, Subject-Verb Pair, Preposition, Prepositional Phrase
2	Conjunction, Coordinating Conjunction
3	Clause, Dependent Clause, www Word
4	Sentence Openers, #3 -ly Adverb Opener
5	#4 -ing Opener, Quotation, Apostrophes, Verb, Linking Verb, Helping Verb
6	Adjective, Commas with Adjectives before a Noun
7	Interjection
10	Run-On
11	Noun
12	Pronoun
13	Indefinite Pronoun
14	Number Words and Numerals
15	Adverb
18	Title
25	Comparative and Superlative Adjectives and Adverbs

Scope and Sequence

Week numbers indicate when a concept is introduced or specifically reinforced in a lesson. Once introduced the concept is practiced throughout the book.

Parts of Speech

Concept	Weeks
Noun	11, 25
Pronoun	12, 13, 18, 25
Preposition	1, 14
Verb	5, 24
Conjunction	
coordinating conjunction	2, 20, 27
subordinating conjunction	3
Adjective	6, 15, 25, 26
Adverb	15
Interjection	7

Capitalization

Concept	Weeks
First Word of Sentence	1
Proper Noun	1
Proper Adjective	1
Personal Pronoun I	1
Title	1
Quotation Marks	5, 10, 27
Noun of Direct Address	5
Interjection	7
Literary Titles	18

Punctuation

Concept	Weeks
End Marks	1, 5, 10
quote	5, 10, 27
interjection	7
attribution	10, 27
Commas	
prepositional phrase	1
coordinating conjunction	2, 10
dependent clause	3, 7, 16
sentence adverb	4
sentence openers	4, 5
quotation marks	5, 10
noun of direct address	5
phrases	1, 7, 8

Institute for Excellence in Writing *Fix It! Grammar: Frog Prince Student Book Level 5*

Week	1	2	3	4	5	6	7	8	9	10	11	12	13	14	15	16	17	18	19	20	21	22	23	24	25	26	27	28	29	30

Commas, cont.

adjectives						6																								
interjection							7																							
unnecessary commas									9																			28		
comma splice										10																				
contrasting items																					21									
Apostrophe					5																									
Quotation Marks					5					10							17					22					27			
Semicolon										10														24						

Clauses

Main Clause	1		3																											
Dependent Clause			3																											
Who/Which Clause			3				7	8			11				15				19											
That Clause			3											14		16		18												
Adverb Clause			3	4											15	16	17				21									
Adjective Clause															15	16	17					22								

Phrases

Prepositional Phrase	1			4			7							14	15															
Verb Phrase					5																									
Participial (-ing) Phrase					5			8						14	15			18					23							
Appositive											11											22								

Other Concepts

Indentation	1																													
Subject-Verb Pairs	1																													
Numbers														14																
Usage																														
who/whom/whose																			19											
affect/effect																								24						
among/between																									25					
than/then																										26				
accept/except																													29	
Words as Words																						22								

Run-On

	Week	1	2	3	4	5	6	7	8	9	10	11	12	13	14	15	16	17	18	19	20	21	22	23	24	25	26	27	28	29	30
Fused Sentence											10																				
Comma Splice											10																				
Fix																															
period											10	11																			
semicolon											10	11													24						
comma + cc											10	11									20										
adverb clause																						21									

Stylistic Techniques

	Week	1	2	3	4	5	6	7	8	9	10	11	12	13	14	15	16	17	18	19	20	21	22	23	24	25	26	27	28	29	30
Strong Verb		1															16														
Quality Adjective								7								15	16														
Who/Which Clause				3				7				11								19											
-ly Adverb								7								15	16														
Adverb Clause				3												15	16	17				21									
#1 Subject Opener					4																									29	
#2 Prepositional Opener					4			7							14								22							29	
#3 -ly Adverb Opener					4																									29	
#4 -ing Opener						5			8										18					23						29	
#5 Clausal Opener					4																		22							29	
#6 Vss Opener					4																									29	

Vocabulary

1	decorous compassion esteemed devotion	2	obstinate courtiers roe repulsed	3	chic fastidiousness court dwindling	4	charge tractable gratify resemble	5	minuscule conservatory eyeing roamed	6	stately regrettable inconsolable benefactor
7	honored proposed inquisitiveness stipulation	8	retrieve salvage hastily wheezed	9	sumptuously hastened hospitably audacious	10	deficiencies despicable theatrics audibly	11	sire whined integrity complied	12	unceremoniously relish deduced pretentious
13	daunting oblivious decency plummeting	14	humility fated sequestered conjectured	15	substantial inadvertently feigned mortified	16	dangled convalescence sullen resolved	17	imperial marveled proffered hesitantly	18	responded stump reputation suspicious
19	ignobly futilely hampering brimming	20	evaded brandished prominent gallant	21	mourned bona fide snickered testily	22	toady repulsive pattered luster	23	commiserate humane regaled demeanor	24	odious chastise empathy discontent
25	rummaged precise mute emphatically	26	credible undaunted mere noxious	27	agitated parched detect jiggled	28	callously insubordination grievingly laborious	29	arrogant contritely coveted entrusting	30	poignantly abhorrent remorse reversed

Institute for Excellence in Writing *Fix It! Grammar: Frog Prince Student Book Level 5*

Contents

Weekly Lessons

Week 1	1	Week 16	91
Week 2	7	Week 17	97
Week 3	13	Week 18	103
Week 4	19	Week 19	109
Week 5	25	Week 20	115
Week 6	31	Week 21	121
Week 7	37	Week 22	127
Week 8	43	Week 23	133
Week 9	49	Week 24	139
Week 10	55	Week 25	145
Week 11	61	Week 26	151
Week 12	67	Week 27	157
Week 13	73	Week 28	163
Week 14	79	Week 29	169
Week 15	85	Week 30	175

Appendices

Appendix I: Complete Story
- Frog Prince 185

Appendix II: Collection Pages
- -ly Adverb 195
- Strong Verb 197
- Quality Adjective 199

Appendix III: Lists
- Pronoun 201
- Preposition, Verb, Conjunction 202
- Clause 203
- Phrase 204
- Sentence Opener 205

Learn It!

Week 1

Capitalization
Capitalize the first word of a sentence.
Capitalize proper nouns and proper adjectives.
Capitalize the personal pronoun *I*.
Capitalize a title when it is used with a person's name.

Titles capitalized before a person's name include mister and missus as well as job titles like doctor, king, and president.

The king was King Morton.

End Mark
Use a period at the end of a statement.
Use a question mark at the end of a question.
Use an exclamation mark at the end of a sentence that expresses strong emotion.

Indentation
An **indentation** shows the start of a new paragraph. In fiction (stories) there are four reasons to start a new paragraph: new speaker, new topic, new place, new time.

Fix It! Place three short lines below letters that should be capitalized.
Draw a slanted line through letters that should be lowercase.
Place the correct end mark at the end of each sentence.
Add the ¶ symbol (known as a pilcrow) in front of each sentence that should start a new paragraph. When you rewrite the passage, indent. Start the sentence on the next line and write ½ inch from the left margin.

¶ Dorinda's new dress cost king morton an outrageous amount of money. The King was not pleased!

Subject and Verb
A **verb** shows action, links the subject to another word, or helps another verb. Every verb has a subject. The subject and verb (*s v*) belong together.
A **subject** is a noun or pronoun that performs a verb action. It tells who or what the clause is about.

Verb Test:
I _____ .
It _____ .

Verb Lists: Appendix III

Main Clause
A **main clause** contains a subject and a verb and expresses a complete thought, so it can stand alone as a sentence. Every sentence must have a main clause.

Find It! Read the sentence and look for the verb.
Ask, "Who or what _____ (verb)?"

Mark It! Write *v* above each verb and *s* above each subject.
Place square brackets around the main clause *[MC]*.

[King Morton ruled wisely].
   s   v

MC Main Clause

Contains: subject + verb
stands alone

Clause Overview: Appendix III

Strong Verb
A **strong verb** dresses up writing because it creates a strong image or feeling. A strong verb is an action verb, never a linking or a helping verb. Look for strong verbs in this book and write them on the Strong Verb collection page, Appendix II.

Institute for Excellence in Writing *Fix It! Grammar: Frog Prince* Student Book Level 5

8 Parts of Speech

Preposition

Definition:
A preposition starts a phrase that shows the relationship between a noun or pronoun and another word in the sentence.

Pattern:
preposition + noun
(no verb)

List:
Appendix III

Phrase Overview:
Appendix III

Prepositional Phrase

A **prepositional phrase** begins with a preposition and ends with a noun or pronoun, which is called the object of the preposition.

A **preposition** is the first word in a prepositional phrase. It shows the relationship between its object (a noun or pronoun) and another word in the sentence. Review the prepositions in Appendix III.

An **object of the preposition** is the last word in a prepositional phrase. It is always a noun or pronoun.

A prepositional phrase adds imagery or information to a sentence because the entire phrase functions as an adjective describing a noun or as an adverb modifying a verb or an adjective.

Formal gardens near a large conservatory featured exotic plants.

Near is the first word in the prepositional phrase. *Near* is a preposition. *Conservatory* is the noun at the end of the prepositional phrase. It is the object of the preposition.

Near shows the relationship between conservatory (its object) and gardens (another word in the sentence). *Near* tells which gardens featured exotic plants. They are not the gardens behind, inside, or past a large conservatory. They are the gardens near a large conservatory.

The king's daughters often explored the gardens with him.

With is the first word in the prepositional phrase. *With* is a preposition. *Him* is the pronoun at the end of the prepositional phrase. It is the object of the preposition.

When a personal pronoun follows a preposition and functions as the object of the preposition, use an objective case pronoun. It is incorrect to write *with I* or *with he* because *I* and *he* are not objective case pronouns.

		Objective Case
		object of preposition
singular	1st	me
	2nd	you
	3rd	him, her, it
plural	1st	us
	2nd	you
	3rd	them

, If a prepositional opener has five words or more, follow it with a comma.

If two or more prepositional phrases open a sentence, follow the last phrase with a comma.

✗ Do not put a comma in front of a prepositional phrase.

Mark It!   Underline each prepositional phrase.
Write ***prep*** above the preposition.
Write ***op*** above the object of the preposition.

Fix It!   Insert or remove commas. Follow the comma rules.

        prep   op   prep   op
In a charming ancient castle, [King Morton lived with his daughters].

                         prep op
[They dined, with him].

Do not include the opener in the main clause square brackets.

Week 1
Day 1

Read It!   **Mark It!**   **Fix It!**

Complete the passage in this order: Read It! Mark It! Fix It!

1 vocabulary

5 prepositional phrases
2 [main clauses]
2 subject-verb pairs (s v)

1 indent
5 capitals
3 commas
1 end mark

In the recent past, in an obscure Kingdom, among the alps a **decorous** King reigned faithfully. His family line of monarchs stretched back to the middle ages

Rewrite It! _____

Read It!	Mark It!	Fix It!	Week 1
1 vocabulary	3 <u>prepositional phrases</u> 2 [main clauses] 2 subject-verb pairs (s v)	3 capitals 2 commas 1 end mark	Day 2

King Morton had inherited the Throne, from his Father nearly three decades before. Like his Father, King Morton ruled fairly and showed **compassion** to all

Rewrite It! _____

Read It!	Mark It!	Fix It!	Week 1
1 vocabulary	3 prepositional phrases	4 capitals	Day 3
	3 [main clauses]	1 comma	
	3 subject-verb pairs (s v)	1 end mark	

As a kindhearted Ruler, King Morton loved his subjects. The people, of the land **esteemed** him. maribella and dorinda, the King's daughters, lived with him

Rewrite It! _____

Read It!	Mark It!	Fix It!	Week 1
1 vocabulary	2 <u>prepositional phrases</u> 2 [main clauses] 2 subject-verb pairs (s v)	1 capital 1 comma 1 end mark	Day 4

Everyone in the land admired his **devotion**, to his girls.

his younger daughter, however, frustrated him greatly

Rewrite It!

Learn It!

Week 2

Conjunction

A **conjunction** connects words, phrases, or clauses. A **coordinating conjunction** (cc) connects the same type of words, phrases, or clauses. The items must be grammatically the same: two or more adjectives, two or more prepositional phrases, two or more main clauses, and so forth. Use the acronym FANBOYS to remember the coordinating conjunctions.

> The staff served King Morton, Princess Dorinda, and Princess Maribella.

And connects three nouns: *King Morton, Princess Dorinda,* and *Princess Maribella.*

> ❜ Use commas to separate three or more items in a series.
> **PATTERN a, b, and c**

> The king lived in the castle with his daughters and with the staff.

And connects two prepositional phrases: *with his daughters* and *with the staff.*

> ✗ Do not use a comma before a cc when it connects two items in a series unless they are main clauses.
> **PATTERN a and b**

> Dorinda raced through the gardens, and Maribella collected daisies.

And connects two main clauses. A subject and verb pair (Dorinda raced) comes before the coordinating conjunction, and a subject and verb pair (Maribella collected) comes after. When a subject and verb pair follows the coordinating conjunction, use a comma.

> ❜ Use a comma before a cc when it connects two main clauses.
> **PATTERN MC, cc MC**

Compare the last sentence to this sentence:

> Dorinda raced through the gardens and collected daisies.

And connects two verbs: *raced* and *collected.* A subject and verb (Dorinda raced) come before the coordinating conjunction, but only a verb (collected) comes after. The verbs have the same subject. This is the same pattern as **a and b** when *a* and *b* are verbs.

> ✗ Do not use a comma before a cc when it connects two verbs.
> **PATTERN MC cc 2nd verb**

Mark It! Write *cc* above each coordinating conjunction.

Fix It! Insert or remove commas. Follow the comma rules.

>   cc
> Dorinda ran through the gardens, smelled the roses, and picked daisies.

>   cc
> Dorinda was lovely, but spoiled. [remove comma]

>   cc
> Maribella sketched the flowers, and Dorinda bounced a ball.

>   cc
> The king groaned at Dorinda's mischief, yet loved her anyway. [remove comma]

---

8 Parts of Speech

Coordinating Conjunction

Definition:
A coordinating conjunction connects the same type of words, phrases, or clauses.

FANBOYS

for, and, nor, but, or, yet, so

❜ a, b, and c

✗ a and b

❜ MC, cc MC

✗ MC cc 2nd verb

Institute for Excellence in Writing *Fix It! Grammar: Frog Prince* Student Book Level 5   7

Coordinating Conjunctions
Figure out what is wrong with the following sentences.
Consider what the coordinating conjunction is connecting.
　Rewrite the sentences correctly.

Dorinda cried out but when she pricked her finger on the thorn.

_____

_____

The sisters argued then they reunited.

_____

_____

Mud splattered her dress and was ruined.

_____

_____

Dorinda teased Maribella, but Maribella laughed, and the sisters argued, yet they hugged each other in the end.

_____

_____

Week 2
Day 1

Read It!   **Mark It!**   **Fix It!**

Complete the passage in this order: Read It! Mark It! Fix It!

1 vocabulary

1 coordinating conjunction (cc)
3 prepositional phrases
2 [main clauses]
2 subject-verb pairs (s v)

1 indent
3 commas
1 end mark

Princess Dorinda had been an **obstinate** child, from toddlerhood. As a child, she often escaped from the nursery, and found mischief

Rewrite It! _____

_____

_____

_____

Week 2
Day 2

Read It!

1 vocabulary

Mark It!

1 coordinating conjunction (cc)
4 prepositional phrases
1 [main clause]
1 subject-verb pair (s v)

Fix It!

2 capitals
4 commas
1 end mark

She once stole, into the Throne Room swung on the chandeliers and landed, at the feet of the scandalized **courtiers**

Rewrite It! _____

Read It!	Mark It!	Fix It!	Week 2
1 vocabulary	1 coordinating conjunction (cc)	1 capital	Day 3
	2 prepositional phrases	3 commas	
	2 [main clauses]	1 end mark	
	2 subject-verb pairs (s v)		

On another occasion, she upset the prestigious new chef, and her staff. They were experimenting, with Sturgeon **roe** ice cream

Rewrite It!

Week 2
Day 4

Read It!

1 vocabulary

Mark It!

3 coordinating conjunctions (cc)
3 <u>prepositional phrases</u>
2 [main clauses]
2 subject-verb pairs (s v)

Fix It!

3 commas
1 end mark

Dorinda sneaked a taste, and expected a sweet treat but instead of bits of chocolate the taste of salty fish eggs first surprised and then **repulsed** her

Rewrite It! _____

Week 3

Learn It!

Clause
A **clause** is a group of related words that contains both a subject and a verb.

Clause Overview: Appendix III

Main Clause
Week 1 you learned that a **main clause** contains a subject and a verb and expresses a complete thought.

          s   v
[Dorinda's dress was expensive].
  Every sentence must have a main clause.

          s   v   s   v
[Dorinda's dress was expensive], and [this frustrated her father].
  Two main clauses can be placed in the same sentence if they are connected with a comma and a coordinating conjunction. **MC, cc MC**

MC Main Clause

Contains:
subject + verb

stands alone

Dependent Clause
A **dependent clause** contains a subject and a verb but does not express a complete thought. It cannot stand alone as a sentence but must have a main clause before or after it. In this book you will mark three types of dependent clauses.

DC Dependent Clause

Who/Which Clause
              w/w   s   v
[Dorinda's dress, (which she purchased online), was expensive].

Contains:
subject + verb

cannot stand alone

Who/Which **Clause**

First Word:
who or which

Commas:
unless essential

Marking:
w/w

A *who/which* **clause** is a dependent clause that begins with *who* or *which*. It is an adjective clause because it follows the noun it describes. Use the pronoun *who* when referring to people, personified animals, and pets. Use the pronoun *which* when referring to things, animals, and places.

The subject of most *who/which* clauses is *who* or *which*, but sometimes the subject is another word in the clause.

When the first word of either a *who* or a *which* clause functions as an adjective, use *whose*. *Whose* is a possessive case pronoun, which functions as an adjective to show ownership.

  , Place commas around a *who/which* clause if it is nonessential.

  ✗ Do not place commas around a *who/which* clause if it is essential (changes the meaning of the sentence).

Weeks 3–6 contain only nonessential *who/which* clauses. They require commas. Week 7 you will learn how to determine if a clause is essential or nonessential.

That Clause
                  that   s   v
[It frustrated the king] (that Dorinda purchased the dress).

That **Clause**

Pattern:
that + subject + verb

First Word:
that

Commas:
none

Marking:
that

A *that* **clause** is a dependent clause that begins with the word *that* and contains a subject and a verb. Because *that* clauses are essential to the sentence, they do not take commas.

  ✗ *That* clauses do not take commas.

Institute for Excellence in Writing *Fix It! Grammar: Frog Prince* Student Book Level 5

Adverb Clause

Pattern:
www word + subject + verb

First Word:
www word

Commas:
after, not before

Marking:
AC

Adverb Clause

```
        AC              s    v              v
(Although Dorinda did not need another dress), [she
                    AC         s   v
purchased this one] (because it had real gold).
```

An **adverb clause** is a dependent clause that begins with a www word (a subordinating conjunction) and contains a subject and a verb.

The acronym *www.asia.b* reminds you of the eight most common www words. However, these are not the only words that begin an adverb clause. Other words can function as www words too.

Memorize It!   when   while   where   as   since   if   although   because
after   before   until   unless   whenever   whereas   than

A www word must have a subject and verb after it to begin an adverb clause.

> Use a comma after an adverb clause that comes before a main clause.
> **PATTERN AC, MC**

> Do not use a comma before an adverb clause.
> **PATTERN MC AC**

Mark It! and Fix It!

Recognizing the basic clause and phrase structures in a sentence will help you punctuate sentences properly. Label the subject-verb pairs to determine how many clauses are in each sentence. Focus on the word that begins the clause to determine if it is a dependent clause or a main clause. After you have identified each clause, check its placement in the sentence and follow the comma rules.

Mark It!   Place parentheses around the dependent clause.
Write *v* above each verb and *s* above each subject.
Identify the dependent clause by looking at the first word of the clause.
Write *w/w* above the word *who*, *which*, or *whose*.
Write *that* above the word *that*.
Write *AC* above the *www* word.

Fix It!   Insert or remove commas. Follow the comma rules.

```
                   w/w            s      v
[King Morton, (whose castle was vast), had lost his crown].

                               that   s   v
[It frustrated the king], (that he had lost his crown).

                              AC    s   v
[The king was irritable], (since he had lost his crown).
```

Week 3
Day 1

Read It! **Mark It!** **Fix It!**

Complete the passage in this order: Read It! Mark It! Fix It!

1 vocabulary

1 coordinating conjunction (cc)
3 prepositional phrases
1 [main clause]
1 who/which clause (w/w)
1 adverb clause (AC)
3 subject-verb pairs (s v)

1 indent
1 capital
5 commas
1 end mark

The princess who had earned a reputation for beauty considered herself quite **chic**, because she wore her hair, in a french twist, and had a beauty spot on her cheek

Rewrite It!

Week 3
Day 2

Read It!	Mark It!	Fix It!
1 vocabulary	1 coordinating conjunction (cc)	1 indent
	2 <u>prepositional phrases</u>	1 capital
	2 [main clauses]	2 commas
	1 *that* clause (that)	1 end mark
	3 subject-verb pairs (s v)	

Her beauty was flawed by her reputation for **fastidiousness**, and self-centeredness. King Morton hoped, that she would consider several young Suitors

Rewrite It! _____

Read It!	Mark It!	Fix It!	Week 3
1 vocabulary	2 coordinating conjunctions (cc)	1 capital	Day 3
	2 prepositional phrases	4 commas	
	3 [main clauses]	1 end mark	
	3 subject-verb pairs (s v)		

Dorinda refused them time after time yet they continued to **court** her. None were wealthy handsome or Titled enough, for her highness

Rewrite It!

Read It!	Mark It!	Fix It!
1 vocabulary	1 coordinating conjunction (cc)	3 commas
	1 <u>prepositional phrase</u>	1 end mark
	1 [main clause]	
	1 *who/which* clause (w/w)	
	1 adverb clause (AC)	
	3 subject-verb pairs (s v)	

Week 3
Day 4

King Morton whose patience was **dwindling** shook his head in despair, and sighed deeply when his daughter voiced her desires

Rewrite It! _____

Learn It!

Week 4

Sentence Opener

A **sentence opener** is a descriptive word, phrase, or clause that is added to the beginning of a sentence. Using different sentence openers makes writing more interesting.

Sentence Opener List: Appendix III

#1 Subject Opener

①   S   V
[The tired governess wondered how to teach Dorinda].

① subject

A **#1 subject opener** is a sentence that begins with the subject of the sentence. Sometimes an article or adjective will come before the subject, but the sentence is still a #1 subject opener.

#2 Prepositional Opener

②
Before the queen's unfortunate death, [Constance served the queen].
②
At the encouragement of the king, [Constance cared for the girls].

② prepositional

Pattern:
preposition + noun
(no verb)

comma if 5+ words

A **#2 prepositional opener** is a sentence that begins with a prepositional phrase. The first word in the sentence must be a preposition.

> If a prepositional opener has five words or more, follow it with a comma.
> If two or more prepositional phrases open a sentence, follow the last phrase with a comma.

#3 -ly Adverb Opener

③ -ly
Clearly, [Dorinda embarrassed Lady Constance].
③ -ly
Secretly [Constance enjoyed Dorinda's spunk].

③ -ly adverb

comma if -ly adverb modifies sentence

(It was ___ that ___.)

A **#3 -ly adverb opener** is a sentence that begins with an -ly adverb.

> Use a comma if an -ly adverb opener modifies the sentence.

✗ Do not use a comma if an -ly adverb opener modifies the verb.

To determine if an -ly adverb modifies the sentence, test it: It was ___ that ___ .
  If this makes sense, the -ly adverb is a sentence adverb. Use a comma.
  If this does not make sense, confirm that the -ly adverb modifies the verb.
  Do not use a comma.

⑤ clausal

Pattern:
www word + subject + verb

comma after clause
AC, MC

#5 Clausal Opener

⑤ AC s v
(Although Dorinda disregarded regal protocol as a child**),** [Constance expected more from the princess].

A **#5 clausal opener** is a sentence that begins with an adverb clause. The #5 clausal opener will always have a comma and a main clause after it.

❜ Use a comma after an adverb clause that comes before a main clause.
PATTERN AC, MC

#6 Vss Opener

⑥ s v
[Lady Constance needed a miracle].

⑥ vss

2–5 words

has main clause

A **# 6 vss opener** is a very short sentence. *Very short* means two to five words. *Sentence* means it must have a main clause.

Mark It! and Fix It!

Starting this week, you will mark five of the six sentence openers. Number every sentence opener except questions and quoted sentences.

Mark It! Determine the type of opener that begins the sentence and number it. Number the openers after the passage has been marked and fixed.

Fix It! Insert or remove commas. Follow the comma rules.

① s v
[The young princess counted the days until her birthday].

②
For her birthday**,** [Dorinda received a golden ball].

③ -ly
Oddly**,** [Dorinda tried to bounce the precious ball].

⑤ AC s v v
(Because the ball was made of gold**),** [it would not bounce].

⑥ s v
[King Morton raged].

Sometimes it appears that more than one sentence opener begins a sentence. When this happens, place the comma after the last opener. Number the sentence opener based on the first word of the sentence.

Read It!	Mark It!	Fix It!	Week 4
			Day 1

Number the sentence openers after the passage has been marked and fixed.

1 vocabulary

3 prepositional phrases
2 [main clauses]
1 *who/which* clause (w/w)
3 subject-verb pairs (s v)
2 openers

1 indent
4 commas

Clearly Dorinda annoyed many, in the palace.

Lady Constance who had cared for her since childhood had virtually stopped training her young **charge**.

Rewrite It! _____

Read It!	Mark It!	Fix It!	Week 4
1 vocabulary	1 coordinating conjunction (cc)	3 commas	Day 2
	2 prepositional phrases		
	2 [main clauses]		
	1 adverb clause (AC)		
	3 subject-verb pairs (s v)		
	2 openers		

Although Dorinda had seemed a lovable **tractable** and contented child in her youth many years of indulgence had spoiled her. She complained constantly.

Rewrite It!

Read It!	Mark It!	Fix It!	Week 4
			Day 3
1 vocabulary	2 coordinating conjunctions (cc)	1 capital	
	2 <u>prepositional phrases</u>	3 commas	
	3 [main clauses]		
	1 adverb clause (AC)		
	4 subject-verb pairs (s v)		
	2 openers		

Unfortunately no expense had been spared to **gratify** the two girls when the girl's Mother was alive. They enjoyed custom dolls with complete wardrobes, and assorted furniture but they always asked for more.

Rewrite It!

Week 4

Day 4

Read It!	Mark It!	Fix It!
1 vocabulary	1 coordinating conjunction (cc)	1 capital
	1 prepositional phrase	5 commas
	2 [main clauses]	
	1 *that* clause (that)	
	2 adverb clauses (AC)	
	5 subject-verb pairs (s v)	
	2 openers	

When they were young girls they were disappointed, that their fairy-tale playground did not **resemble** Cinderella's Castle. As a teenager, Dorinda stomped her foot, and pouted, when a new television was delivered.

Rewrite It! _____

Learn It!

Week 5

Sentence Opener

A **sentence opener** is a descriptive word, phrase, or clause that is added to the beginning of a sentence. Number every sentence opener except questions and quoted sentences.

Sentence Opener List: Appendix III

#4 -ing Opener

④   s   v
Rolling her eyes, [Dorinda ignored her father].

④ -ing

Pattern:
-ing word/phrase, main clause

comma after phrase

A **#4 -ing opener** begins with a participle, a verb form that ends in -ing. The -ing opener usually includes additional words that form a phrase. *Rolling* is the participle. *Rolling her eyes* is the participial phrase. The entire phrase functions as an adjective. *Rolling her eyes* describes *Dorinda*.

The thing after the comma must be the thing doing the inging. *Dorinda* is the thing (subject of main clause) after the comma. *Dorinda* is doing the *rolling*.

❞ Use a comma after an -ing opener, even if it is short.
PATTERN -ing word/phrase, main clause

Quotation Marks

"My ball rolled away," the princess cried.

Quotation marks indicate words are spoken. The quote is the sentence in quotation marks. The attribution is the person speaking and the speaking verb. If a quote has an attribution, the attribution may precede, interrupt, or follow the quote.

Capitalize the first word of the quote. Capitalize the first word of the attribution if it is the first word of the sentence.

Place quotation marks around the words that are spoken. Separate an attribution from a direct quote with a comma. If a direct quote is a question or exclamation, follow with a ? or !.

❞ Use a comma to separate an attribution from a direct quote.

Attribution, "Quote."
"Quote," attribution.

"Quote," attribution, "rest of quoted sentence."

Attribution, "Quote?"
"Quote?" attribution.

Attribution, "Quote!"
"Quote!" attribution.

Noun of Direct Address

"Dorinda, [will you toss the ball outdoors]?"

A **noun of direct address** (NDA) is a noun used to directly address someone. It only appears in a quoted sentence. Capitalize a title used as an NDA with the exceptions of *sir* and *madam*. In the example *Dorinda* is the NDA.

❞ Place commas around a noun of direct address.

Apostrophe

The sisters agreed. "Let's sit on Dad's throne!"

An **apostrophe** indicates that letters are missing in a contraction (Let's) or shows ownership with a possessive adjective. To form a singular possessive adjective, add an apostrophe + s to a noun: Dad's. To form a plural possessive adjective when the noun ends in s, add an apostrophe after the s: girls'. If the plural noun does not end in s, add an apostrophe + s: children's.

8 Parts of Speech

Verb

Definition:
A verb shows action, links the subject to another word, or helps another verb.

Verb Test:
I _____ .
It _____ .

Linking Verbs
  Be verbs
  seem, become, appear, grow, remain, taste, sound, smell, feel, look

  linking verb + noun
  linking verb + adjective

Helping Verbs
  Be verbs
  have, has, had, do, does, did, may, might, must, can, will, shall, could, would, should

  helping verb(s) + main verb (action or linking)

Be Verbs
  am, is, are, was, were, be, being, been

Verb Lists: Appendix III

Verb

Every verb has a subject. A verb acts alone or in phrases to perform different actions.

Action Verb

Dorinda had a golden ball. She tossed it into the air.

An **action verb** (*av*) shows action or ownership.
Had shows ownership. *Tossed* shows action.

Linking Verb

Dorinda was a princess. She appeared spoiled.

A **linking verb** (*lv*) links the subject to a noun or to an adjective.
Was is a linking verb that links the subject *Dorinda* to the noun *princess*. The noun *princess* follows the linking verb and renames the subject, the word *Dorinda*.
Appeared is a linking verb that links the subject *She* to the adjective *spoiled*. The adjective *spoiled* follows the linking verb and describes the subject, the word *she*.

Helping Verb

Dorinda had tossed the ball. She could appear spoiled.

A **helping verb** (*hv*) helps an action verb or a linking verb. The helping verb and the verb it helps (action or linking) form a verb phrase.
Had is a helping verb that helps the action verb *tossed*. You know *had* is a helping verb because a verb follows it. The verb phrase *had tossed* shows action.
Could is a helping verb that helps the linking verb *appear*. You know *could* is a helping verb because a verb follows it. The verb phrase *could appear* links the subject *She* to the adjective *spoiled*.

Mark It! Mark every verb as an action verb (*av*), linking verb (*lv*), or helping verb (*hv*).

```
       s   v              v        s   v
           hv            av            lv
The gold ball would not bounce. It was too heavy.
```

Think About It!

Be verbs can be linking verbs or helping verbs. If a *be* verb has a noun or an adjective after it, it is a linking verb. If a *be* verb has another verb after it, it is a helping verb.
  The round gold object was (lv) a ball (n). It was (lv) heavy (adj).
  The ball was (hv) thrown (av) into the air.

Many linking verbs can be linking or action verbs. If you can substitute *is* for the verb, it is a linking verb. If you cannot, it is an action verb.
  Ice cream tasted sweet. Substitute *is*: Ice cream is sweet. *Tasted* is a linking verb.
  She tasted the ice cream. Substitute *is*: She is the ice cream. *Tasted* is an action verb.

Many helping verbs can be helping or action verbs. If a verb on the helping verb list has a verb after it, the first verb is a helping verb. If it does not, it is an action verb.
  Dorinda had (av) a golden ball. A verb does not follow *had*.
  Dorinda had (hv) tossed (av) the ball. *Tossed* follows *had*.

Read It! **Mark It!** **Fix It!**

Week 5
Day 1

Continue to underline the prepositional phrases. However, you no longer need to mark *prep* and *op*. From now on, number the sentence openers after the passage has been marked and fixed.

1 vocabulary

1 coordinating conjunction (cc)
2 prepositional phrases
2 [main clauses]
2 adverb clauses (AC)
4 subject-verb pairs (s v)
2 openers

5 commas
1 apostrophe

Declaring it **minuscule** she demanded a theater room with sound lighting and comfort. Although Lady Constance did not approve she met Dorindas demands, because she did not want to argue with her.

Rewrite It!

Week 5
Day 2

Read It!	**Mark It!**	**Fix It!**

1 vocabulary	4 prepositional phrases	1 indent
2 [main clauses]	4 commas
1 *who/which* clause (w/w)	1 apostrophe
3 subject-verb pairs (s v)
2 openers

On a crisp spring morning Princess Dorinda played, with her latest plaything which was a golden ball. Tossing it up she wandered among the plant's in the **conservatory**.

Rewrite It! _____

Week 5
Day 3

Read It!	Mark It!	Fix It!
1 vocabulary	1 coordinating conjunction (cc)	1 indent
	2 prepositional phrases	1 capital
	3 [main clauses]	5 commas
	3 subject-verb pairs (s v)	1 end mark
	2 openers	2 quotation marks
		1 apostrophe

From a distance, the King observed his daughter, and her golden ball. **Eyeing** the glass windows he suggested Dorinda why dont you toss that ball in the garden.

Rewrite It! _____

Week 5
Day 4

Read It!
1 vocabulary

Mark It!
2 coordinating conjunctions (cc)
3 prepositional phrases
3 [main clauses]
3 subject-verb pairs (s v)
3 openers

Fix It!
1 indent
1 capital
4 commas

Dorinda rolled her eyes. Crossly, she grabbed her stylish boots, and jacket, and went outside. With her ball in hand the Princess **roamed** through the expansive castle gardens.

Rewrite It! _____

Learn It!

Week 6

Adjective

An **adjective** describes a noun or a pronoun. It can come before the noun it describes (*charming* princess), or it can follow a linking verb and describe the subject of the clause (princess was *charming*).

Often, two or more adjectives come before a noun. If the consecutive adjectives are cumulative adjectives, do not use a comma. If they are coordinate adjectives, use a comma.

Adjectives can be grouped into categories.

Categories	Some Examples		
quantity	two	several	few
opinion	careless	unfortunate	spoiled
size	deep	heavy	narrow
age	new	young	ancient
shape	round	angular	square
color	red	blue	brunette
origin	European	Catholic	imperial
material	gold	stone	cotton
purpose	frying (pan)	throne (room)	shade (tree)

8 Parts of Speech

Adjective

Definition:
An adjective describes a noun or pronoun.

Test:
the _____ pen

Questions:
 which one?
 what kind?
 how many?
 whose?

Cumulative Adjectives

     adj   *adj*   *n*
The heavy gold ball did not bounce.

Cumulative adjectives build on each other. The first adjective describes the second adjective and the noun that follows. Cumulative adjectives are arranged in a specific order: quantity, opinion, size, age, shape, color, origin, material, purpose. You cannot reverse their order or add *and* between them.

The first adjective (heavy) describes the second adjective and the noun together (gold ball).

It is a gold ball that is heavy. Both the "gold heavy ball" and the "heavy and gold ball" sound strange. *Heavy* and *gold* are cumulative adjectives and do not need a comma.

✗ Do not use a comma to separate cumulative adjectives.

cumulative adjectives build on each other ✗

Coordinate Adjectives

     adj   *adj*   *n*
Dorinda was often a careless, spoiled princess.

Coordinate adjectives independently describe the noun that follows. The adjectives belong in the same category. You can reverse their order or add *and* between them.

Dorinda was both a careless princess and a spoiled princess. Each adjective independently describes the noun.

Both the "spoiled careless princess" and the "careless and spoiled princess" sound correct. *Careless* and *spoiled* are coordinate adjectives and need a comma.

, Use a comma to separate coordinate adjectives.

coordinate adjectives work independently ,

Institute for Excellence in Writing *Fix It! Grammar: Frog Prince* Student Book Level 5

Cumulative or Coordinate?

Two tests help determine whether consecutive adjectives before a noun are cumulative or coordinate.

   Can you reverse their order?
   Can you add *and* between them?
      If you answer no, the adjectives are cumulative. Do not use a comma.
      If you answer yes, the adjectives are coordinate. Use a comma.

Fix It!   Remove the comma between cumulative adjectives.
         Add a comma between coordinate adjectives.

The new, round ball rolled into the deep, narrow well.

Read each sentence and decide if the two adjectives are cumulative or coordinate.
   Circle the correct answer.
   Insert a comma if the adjectives are coordinate.

In the city lived a skillful popular toymaker.

cumulative   **coordinate**

After observing the princesses, he had a strange wonderful idea.

cumulative   **coordinate**

He would design a solid gold ball fit for royalty.

cumulative   **coordinate**

It would be a unique expensive toy.

cumulative   **coordinate**

Of course, it would feel like heavy lead weights.

cumulative   **coordinate**

However, the girls would enjoy rolling it down a smooth brick path.

cumulative   **coordinate**

He never imagined that the ball would roll into the deep dark well.

cumulative   **coordinate**

Read It!	Mark It!	Fix It!	Week 6
			Day 1
1 vocabulary	2 coordinating conjunctions (cc)	1 capital	
	2 prepositional phrases	4 commas	
	1 [main clause]	1 apostrophe	
	1 subject-verb pair (s v)		
	1 opener		

Meandering aimlessly through the **stately**, imperial garden's princess Dorinda repeatedly tossed her ball up, and down, and caught it with slick confidence.

Rewrite It! _____

Week 6

Day 2

Read It!	Mark It!	Fix It!
1 vocabulary	1 coordinating conjunction (cc) 3 prepositional phrases 4 [main clauses] 4 subject-verb pairs (s v) 3 openers	5 commas

At the corner of the well a most **regrettable** event occurred. Carelessly, she tossed her precious, golden ball too high and down it fell, with a splash. Dorinda gasped.

Rewrite It!

34   Institute for Excellence in Writing *Fix It! Grammar: Frog Prince* Student Book Level 5

Read It!	Mark It!	Fix It!	Week 6
1 vocabulary	1 coordinating conjunction (cc)	5 commas	Day 3
	3 prepositional phrases		
	3 [main clauses]		
	1 *who/which* clause (w/w)		
	4 subject-verb pairs (s v)		
	2 openers		

The heavy ball sank to the bottom of the deep dark well. Angry salty tears flowed and Dorinda who was **inconsolable** stomped her foot, in frustration.

Rewrite It!

Week 6

Read It! | **Mark It!** | **Fix It!** | Day 4

1 vocabulary

3 [main clauses]
1 adverb clause (AC)
4 subject-verb pairs (s v)

1 indent
1 comma
2 end marks
4 quotation marks
1 apostrophe

Ive lost my golden baaall Dorinda wailed.

I would reward my **benefactor** handsomely,

if only I could have my ball back

Rewrite It!

Learn It!

Transitional Prepositional Phrases

②

Of course, Dorinda didn't hear since she was distracted.

Dorinda didn't hear, of course, since she was distracted.

Dorinda was distracted, of course.

> Prepositional phrases that function as transitions require commas.
>
> in fact
> in addition
> by the way
> by contrast
> for example
> for instance
> of course
> on the other hand

Week 1 you learned that short prepositional openers do not take commas. You also learned that you should not place commas in front of prepositional phrases. Transitions, however, do take commas. Therefore, when a prepositional phrase functions as a transition, use commas regardless of where the transitional prepositional phrase appears in the sentence.

, Place commas around a transitional prepositional phrase.

Interjection

Wow! It weighs a ton. Oh, it's not that heavy.

An **interjection** expresses an emotion. When it expresses a strong emotion, use an exclamation mark and capitalize the word that follows. When it does not express a strong emotion, use a comma.

Interrogative Pronoun

    S   V

[What happened to the ball]?

An **interrogative pronoun** is used to ask a question. The most common interrogative pronouns are *what, whatever, which, whichever, who, whoever, whom, whose*.

Think About It!

When the pronouns *who, whom, whose,* and *which* function as interrogative pronouns, they ask a question. The question is a main clause and expresses a complete thought.

[Who will find it]?

When the pronouns *who, whom, whose,* and *which* function as relative pronouns, they begin a *who/which* clause. The *who/which* clause is a dependent clause and describes the noun it follows.

[Dorinda's benefactor will be the person] (who will find it).

Quality Adjective and -ly Adverb

A quality adjective and an -ly adverb are two different ways to dress up writing. Like the strong verb, these stylistic devices create a strong image and feeling. A **quality adjective** is more specific than a weak adjective. A weak adjective is overused, boring, or vague. An **-ly adverb** is used to enhance the meaning of the verb, adjective, or adverb that it modifies.

Look for quality adjectives and -ly adverbs in this book and write them on the collection pages found in Appendix II.

Who/Which Clause

Week 3 you began marking *who/which* clauses. There are two types of *who/which* clauses: nonessential and essential.

Nonessential *Who/Which* Clause

Nonessential W/W
adds information to the sentence
use commas

Frogs, which normally do not speak, enjoy damp places.

A **nonessential *who/which* clause** adds information to a sentence, but the clause is not needed for the rest of the sentence to make sense.

Use commas to show that the added information can be removed from the sentence. The nonessential clause may convey important information, but it will not change the meaning of the rest of the sentence if it is removed.

Place commas around a *who/which* clause if it is nonessential.

Frogs, ~~which normally do not speak~~, enjoy damp places.

Without the *which* clause, the reader still knows that frogs enjoy damp places.

Essential *Who/Which* Clause

Essential W/W
defines the noun it follows
do not use commas

The frog who spoke English was unusual.

An **essential *who/which* clause** defines the noun it follows (in the example, frog). Do not use commas because the essential information about the noun cannot be removed from the sentence. If the essential information about the noun were removed, the overall meaning of the sentence would change.

Do not place commas around a *who/which* clause if it is essential (changes the meaning of the sentence).

The frog ~~who spoke English~~ was unusual.

Without the *who* clause the sentence says the frog was unusual. The reader no longer knows which frog is meant. Removing the clause changes the meaning of the sentence.

Nonessential or Essential?

Commas give the reader permission to remove the clause from the sentence.

To determine if a *who/which* clause is essential, remove it from the sentence.

Does the meaning of the sentence change?

If you answer no, the *who/which* clause is nonessential. Use commas.

If you answer yes, the *who/which* clause is essential. Do not use commas.

Fix It! Add commas to nonessential *who/which* clauses.

Remove commas from essential *who/which* clauses.

w/w s   v
Dorinda, (who was the youngest grandchild), was spoiled.

w/w s   v
The grandchild, (who was born first), was also spoiled.

Read It!	Mark It!	Fix It!	Week 7
1 vocabulary	1 coordinating conjunction (cc)	2 indents	Day 1
	3 prepositional phrases	4 commas	
	4 [main clauses]	2 quotation marks	
	1 *who/which* clause (w/w)	2 apostrophes	
	1 adverb clause (AC)		
	6 subject-verb pairs (s v)		
	2 openers		

I would be **honored** to assist you a throaty voice offered. Instantly, Dorindas tear's dried, as she looked around for the person who was speaking. In fact she could turn her tears on and off on a whim.

Rewrite It!

Week 7

Day 2

Read It!   **Mark It!**   **Fix It!**

1 vocabulary

3 prepositional phrases
4 [main clauses]
4 subject-verb pairs (s v)
2 openers

1 indent
2 capitals
4 commas
3 end marks
4 quotation marks

Seeing no one, Dorinda asked oh who has **proposed** such a generous thoughtful offer Hopping toward her on the rim of the well an amphibian croaked It was I

Rewrite It! _____

_____

_____

_____

_____

40   Institute for Excellence in Writing *Fix It! Grammar: Frog Prince* Student Book Level 5

Read It!	Mark It!	Fix It!	Week 7
			Day 3
1 vocabulary	1 coordinating conjunction (cc)	1 indent	
	3 prepositional phrases	4 commas	
	4 [main clauses]	1 end mark	
	1 adverb clause (AC)	2 quotation marks	
	5 subject-verb pairs (s v)		
	2 openers		

As she let loose a spine-tingling shriek Dorinda started to run. Of course her **inquisitiveness** got the better of her and she turned back to the frog.

How can you talk Mr. Frog

Rewrite It!

Week 7
Day 4

Read It!
1 vocabulary

Mark It!
1 coordinating conjunction (cc)
3 prepositional phrases
6 [main clauses]
6 subject-verb pairs (s v)

Fix It!
3 indents
4 commas
2 end marks
6 quotation marks
2 apostrophes

Its a long dull story but I might tell it to you in the future. Would you like me to find your ball Yes I would appreciate that Ill gladly do it with one unique **stipulation** the frog responded.

Rewrite It!

Learn It!

Participial Phrase

A **participial phrase** is a phrase that begins with a present participle, an -ing word. Week 5 you learned that a #4 -ing opener is a sentence that begins with a participial (-ing) phrase. Like a *who/which* clause, a participial phrase is an adjective because the entire phrase describes a noun in the sentence.

Phrase Overview: Appendix III

④
Searching for her lost ball, Dorinda stared into the well.

Searching is the -ing word, the present participle. *Searching for her lost ball* is the participial (-ing) phrase.

When a participial phrase begins a sentence (#4 -ing opener), the entire phrase describes the subject of the sentence. This is why the thing (subject of main clause) after the comma must be the thing doing the inging.

Participial (-ing) phrases do not have to begin a sentence. When a participial phrase comes at the end of a sentence, the entire phrase describes a noun in the sentence. If the noun is the word directly before the -ing phrase, do not use a comma.

Dorinda saw her ball *sitting at the bottom of the well.*

Sitting is the -ing word, the present participle. *Sitting at the bottom of the well* is the participial (-ing) phrase. It describes *ball*, the word directly before it. Do not use a comma.

Dorinda stared into the well, *searching for her lost ball.*

Searching is the -ing word, the present participle. *Searching for her lost ball* is the participial (-ing) phrase. It describes *Dorinda*, not the word directly before it. Use a comma.

, | Use a comma when a participial (-ing) phrase comes at the end of a sentence and describes a noun other than the word it follows.

✗ | Do not use a comma when a participial (-ing) phrase comes at the end of a sentence and describes the word it follows.

Think About It!

The placement of a comma can change the meaning of a sentence.

The king watched the visitors sitting on his bench.

Without a comma this sentence means that the visitors were sitting on the king's bench when the king watched them.

The king watched the visitors, sitting on his bench.

With a comma this sentence means that the king was sitting on his bench when he watched the visitors.

Because both a *who/which* clause and a participial phrase function as adjectives, it is easy to convert one to the other.

Dorinda saw her ball sitting at the bottom of the well.

Dorinda saw her ball, which was sitting at the bottom of the well.

Commas or No Commas?

Read each sentence and decide if the *who/which* clause is nonessential or essential.
    If the clause adds information, it is nonessential. Use commas.
        Nonessential: Need commas
    If the clause defines the noun it follows, it is essential. Do not use commas.
        Essential: Eliminate commas

> Commas give the reader permission to remove the clause from the sentence.

The gardens opened to a park which stretched to the city center.

    nonessential   **essential**

In the early morning teenagers who enjoyed rowing visited the lake.

    nonessential   **essential**

White mulberry trees which attracted silk worms lined the perimeter.

    nonessential   **essential**

Stone benches which sat throughout the garden welcomed visitors.

    nonessential   **essential**

Some children who wanted to see the king approached a guard.

    nonessential   **essential**

Read each sentence and decide if the participial phrase at the end of the sentence describes the word if follows.
    If the -ing phrase describes a noun other than the word it follows, use a comma.
    If the -ing phrase describes the word it follows, do not use a comma.

The king's guard talked to the children wishing to see the king.

Some gardeners were near the lake planting fresh flowers.

Near the lake were some gardeners planting fresh flowers.

They talked to a young girl playing with a jump rope.

She saw her mother and left waving as she walked away.

Week 8
Day 1

Read It!	Mark It!	Fix It!
1 vocabulary	1 coordinating conjunction (cc)	1 indent
	2 prepositional phrases	5 commas
	4 [main clauses]	1 end mark
	1 *who/which* clause (w/w)	4 quotation marks
	1 *that* clause (that)	1 apostrophe
	1 adverb clause (AC)	
	7 subject-verb pairs (s v)	

Ill do anything, that you want! My dad will kill me, if I lose that ball which cost him a royal fortune she replied. You must jump in, and **retrieve** my ball sitting at the bottom of the well

Rewrite It! _____

Read It!	Mark It!	Fix It!	Week 8
1 vocabulary	1 coordinating conjunction (cc)	1 indent	Day 2
	4 prepositional phrases	4 commas	
	1 [main clause]	1 end mark	
	1 adverb clause (AC)	2 quotation marks	
	2 subject-verb pairs (s v)	1 apostrophe	

I'll **salvage** your ball if youll allow me to stay for one night in the palace feasting at your, fancy table, and eating, from your own plate

Rewrite It!

Read It!	Mark It!	Fix It!	Week 8
1 vocabulary	1 coordinating conjunction (cc)	2 indents	Day 3
	3 <u>prepositional phrases</u>	7 commas	
	3 [main clauses]	2 quotation marks	
	3 subject-verb pairs (s v)	1 apostrophe	
	2 openers		

Well of course Dorinda responded **hastily**.

The frog hopped into the water disappeared for a few moments and returned holding Dorindas treasure.

Gleefully, Dorinda snatched the wet slippery ball.

Rewrite It!

Week 8
Day 4

Read It! | **Mark It!** | **Fix It!**
1 vocabulary | 2 <u>prepositional phrases</u> | 1 indent
 | 4 [main clauses] | 3 commas
 | 1 *that* clause (that) | 2 quotation marks
 | 5 subject-verb pairs (s v) | 3 apostrophes
 | 2 openers |

Its solid gold he finally **wheezed**. Skipping back to the palace Princess Dorinda didnt hear him pattering behind her. The exhausted amphibian hoped, that Princess Dorindas word was trustworthy.

Rewrite It! _____
_____
_____
_____

Week 9

Review It!

Commas

There is always a reason a comma is necessary. Follow the comma rules.
When two comma rules contradict, follow the rule that says to use a comma.

, The key to adding commas is to think about parts of speech and the structure of your sentences.

Coordinating Conjunction
Use a comma before a cc when it connects two main clauses. **MC, cc MC**
Use commas to separate three or more items in a series. **a, b, and c**

Who/Which Clause
Use commas unless essential.
Essential means it changes the meaning of the sentence.

Participial (-ing) Phrase
Mid-sentence use commas unless essential.
End-sentence use a comma when it describes a noun other than the word directly before it.

Adjectives
Use a comma to separate coordinate adjectives.
Coordinate means you can reverse their order or add *and* between them.

Interjection
Use a comma after an interjection that does not expresses strong emotion.

Noun of Direct Address (NDA)
Use commas.

Quotations
Use a comma to separate an attribution from a direct quote.
"Quote," attribution.
Attribution, "Quote."
"Quote," attribution, "rest of quoted sentence."

Sentence Openers

(2) prepositional — Use a comma if 5 + words or transition.
preposition + noun (no verb)

(3) -ly adverb — Use a comma if an -ly adverb modifies the sentence.
It was ____ that ____.

(4) -ing — Use a comma after the phrase.
-ing word/phrase, main clause

(5) clausal — Use a comma after the clause. **AC, MC**
www word + subject + verb,

✗ Do not use unnecessary commas.

Institute for Excellence in Writing *Fix It! Grammar: Frog Prince* Student Book Level 5   49

Unnecessary Comma Rules

You have now learned several places where commas are unnecessary.

✗ The key to punctuating sentences correctly is to think about parts of speech and the structure of your sentences.

Subject-Verb Pair
> Do not put a comma between a subject and its verb.

Coordinating Conjunction
> Do not use a comma before a cc when it connects two items in a series (unless main clauses). **a and b**
> Do not use a comma before a cc when it connects two verbs. **MC cc 2nd verb**

Prepositional Phrase
> Do not put a comma in front of a prepositional phrase (unless transition).

Who/Which Clause
> Do not use commas when a *who/which* clause is essential.
>> Essential means it changes the meaning of the sentence.

Participial (-ing) Phrase
> Mid-sentence do not use commas when an -ing phrase is essential.
> End-sentence do not use a comma when it describes the word directly before it.

Adverb Clause
> Do not use a comma before an adverb clause that follows a main clause. **MC AC**

That Clause
> Do not use a comma before a *that* clause.

Adjectives
> Do not use a comma to separate cumulative adjectives.
>> Cumulative means the adjectives must be arranged in a specific order.
>> You cannot reverse their order or add *and* between them.

Interjection
> Do not use a comma after an interjection that expresses strong emotion.
>> Use an exclamation mark instead.

Quotations
> Do not use a comma after a quoted question or quoted exclamation.
> The question mark or exclamation mark replaces the comma.
>> "Quote?" attribution.   "Quote!" attribution.

Sentence Openers
> ② prepositional   Do not use a comma if fewer than 5 words.
> ③ -ly adverb   Do not use a comma if an -ly adverb modifies the verb.

, There is always a reason a comma is necessary.
Follow the comma rules.

Read It!	Mark It!	Fix It!	Week 9 Day 1
1 vocabulary	1 coordinating conjunction (cc) 3 prepositional phrases 2 [main clauses] 1 adverb clause (AC) 3 subject-verb pairs (s v) 2 openers	1 indent 4 commas 1 apostrophe	

While the royal family dined **sumptuously** they heard a faint tap, at the castle door. Within moment's, a footman appeared, and delivered a message to Princess Dorinda.

Rewrite It! _____

Week 9
Day 2

Read It!   **Mark It!**   **Fix It!**

1 vocabulary

1 coordinating conjunction (cc)
3 <u>prepositional phrases</u>
5 [main clauses]
1 *that* clause (that)
6 subject-verb pairs (s v)
2 openers

2 indents
2 capitals
5 commas
4 quotation marks

princess he began You have a visitor at the door. Excusing herself from the table Dorinda **hastened** away. She hoped, that the visitor was her new friend for she was eager to eat dessert with her.

Rewrite It! _____
_____
_____
_____
_____

Week 9
Day 3

Read It!	**Mark It!**	**Fix It!**
1 vocabulary	1 coordinating conjunction (cc)	2 indents
	3 prepositional phrases	4 commas
	4 [main clauses]	2 quotation marks
	1 adverb clause (AC)	1 apostrophe
	5 subject-verb pairs (s v)
	2 openers

When she opened the door blood drained from her face. There sat the frog squatting, and looking at Dorinda with sad, huge eye's. You forgot your pledge to treat me **hospitably** he croaked.

Rewrite It!

Week 9
Day 4

Read It!

1 vocabulary

Mark It!

1 coordinating conjunction (cc)
4 [main clauses]
1 *that* clause (that)
1 adverb clause (AC)
6 subject-verb pairs (s v)
2 openers

Fix It!

2 indents
6 commas
1 end mark
2 quotation marks

Dorinda slammed the door. Truthfully she hoped that the **audacious** annoying amphibian would leave forget her promise and never return. Dorinda who knocked King Morton inquired, when she returned.

Rewrite It!

Learn It!

Week 10

Run-On
A **run-on** occurs when a sentence has main clauses that are not connected properly. There are two types of run-ons: fused sentence and comma splice.

> A frog sat on the steps Dorinda looked horrified.

A **fused sentence** is two main clauses placed in one sentence without any punctuation between them.

Fused sentence:
MC MC

> Dorinda was furious, she slammed the door.
> Dorinda told what happened, the king was displeased.

A **comma splice** is two main clauses placed in one sentence with only a comma between them.

Comma Splice:
MC, MC

These patterns are always wrong!

There are three simple ways to fix a run-on.

Period

> A frog sat on the steps. Dorinda looked horrified.

A sentence is an expression of one idea, so if the main clauses are separate ideas, they belong in two separate sentences. Place a period at the end of each main clause. This is the simplest way to fix a run-on.

Fix:
MC. MC.

Semicolon

> Dorinda was furious; she slammed the door.

A semicolon can fix a run-on. However, it cannot always join main clauses. It should only be used when the two main clauses express a single idea and are similar in length or construction. Use a semicolon sparingly.

Fix:
MC; MC.

Comma + CC

> Dorinda told what happened, **and** the king was displeased.

When a coordinating conjunction (cc) best expresses the relationship between the two main clauses, connect the main clauses with a comma and a coordinating conjunction (for, and, nor, but, or, yet, so).

Fix:
MC, cc MC.

> Dorinda told what happened and the king was displeased.

This is grammatically wrong. If you connect two main clauses with a coordinating conjunction, you must place a comma before the coordinating conjunction. The comma without the cc is a comma splice. The coordinating conjunction without a comma is a comma error.

Fix It!
Fix run-on sentences with the best method.

> Dorinda knew she was in trouble. the staff remained silent.

> The butler smirked; a footman sighed.

> Two footmen removed the salad, and two more served the entrée.

This week's Fix It! provides specific directions for fixing run-on sentences.

Quote and Attribution

"I will not serve the frog."

A **quote** is the sentence in quotation marks. Quotation marks surround the quote to show that these are the speaker's exact words.

A quote may be one or more sentences long and must be punctuated correctly with capital letters and end marks. Commas and periods always go inside closing quotation marks. Exclamation marks and question marks go inside closing quotation marks when they are part of the quoted material.

the princess said

An **attribution** is the person speaking and the speaking verb. Although the attribution contains a main clause (subject and verb), it does not express a complete thought. What did the princess say? The quote which tells what the princess said must be in the same sentence as the attribution in order for the sentence to make sense.

An attribution sets up a direct quote. It may may precede, interrupt, or follow the quote. The first word of the attribution is capitalized when the attribution begins the sentence.

Attribution, "Quote."

"Quote," attribution, "rest of quoted sentence."

"Quote," attribution.

Attribution, "Quote?"

"Quote?" attribution.

Attribution, "Quote!"

"Quote!" attribution.

MC   MC
[The princess said], "[I will not serve the frog]."

This example contains two clauses: a main clause and a main clause. However, because the quote is *what* the person said, it is a necessary part of the attribution. If you insert a period after *said*, the sentence does not make sense.
What did the princess say? The quote must be in the same sentence in order to make sense. With this pattern, a comma correctly separates the attribution (a main clause) from the quote (a main clause).

MC   MC
"[Must I serve the frog]?" [the princess asked].

When a quoted sentence asks a question or expresses a strong emotion, a question mark or exclamation mark replaces the comma. The attribution is not capitalized when the attribution interrupts or follows the quote because the attribution belongs in the same sentence as the quote.

MC   MC
[The princess wailed for several minutes]. "[I will not serve the frog]."

This example contains two clauses: a main clause and a main clause. Because *Dorinda wailed for several minutes* expresses a complete thought, it is not an attribution. Both main clauses require end marks.

MC   that
[The princess said] (that she would not serve the frog).

This example contains two clauses: a main clause and a *that* clause. Together the two clauses express a complete thought. Because *that she would not serve the frog* is not the speaker's direct words but an indirect quote, quotation marks are not used. An indirect quote is a paraphrase of what someone said and uses third-person pronouns and past tense verbs.

Read It!	Mark It!	Fix It!	Week 10
			Day 1
1 vocabulary	1 coordinating conjunction (cc)	2 indents	
	1 prepositional phrase	2 capitals	
	5 [main clauses]	3 commas	
	5 subject-verb pairs (s v)	2 end marks	
	2 openers	4 quotation marks	
		1 apostrophe	
		(fix run-on with period)	

Despite her **deficiencies**, Dorinda truthfully answered her father it was a frog. King Mortons eyes widened and he inquired what did he want

Rewrite It!

Read It!	Mark It!	Fix It!	
1 vocabulary	1 coordinating conjunction (cc)	1 indent	
	2 prepositional phrases	1 capital	
	3 [main clauses]	4 commas	
	3 subject-verb pairs (s v)	2 end marks	
	2 openers	2 quotation marks	
		1 apostrophe	
		(fix run-on with period)	

Crying yet again Dorinda sobbed the story of the frogs considerate rescue, and of her foolish promise she miserably wailed I will not touch that ugly **despicable** thing

Rewrite It!

Read It!	Mark It!	Fix It!	Week 10
1 vocabulary	5 [main clauses] 5 subject-verb pairs (s v) 1 opener	1 indent 1 capital 3 commas 2 end marks 1 semicolon 4 quotation marks 2 apostrophes (fix run-ons with semicolon and period)	Day 3

Dorindas **theatrics** frustrated her father her tear's annoyed him. Daughter he urged you are a royal princess, your word must be trustworthy

Rewrite It!

Week 10

Day 4

Read It!	Mark It!	Fix It!
1 vocabulary	2 prepositional phrases	1 indent
	4 [main clauses]	2 capitals
	4 subject-verb pairs (s v)	4 commas
	2 openers	2 end marks
		2 quotation marks
		(fix run-ons with periods)

Reluctantly, Princess Dorinda slunk to the door, she opened it just wide enough, for the frog to squeeze through you may enter she sighed **audibly**.

Rewrite It! _____

Learn It!

Week 11

Noun and Pronoun Functions

A **noun** names a person, place, thing, or idea. A **pronoun** replaces a noun in order to avoid repetition. Both nouns and pronouns perform many functions (jobs) in a sentence.

    sn   av   do   op   nda   sp lv   pn
The king showed hospitality to the frog. "Frederick, I am King Morton."

Subject

Week 1 you learned that a **subject** is a noun or pronoun that performs a verb action. It tells who or what the clause is about.

    What is the verb? *showed*. Who showed? *king*. *King* is the subject noun (sn) because it tell who the first clause is about.

    What is the verb? *am*. Who am? *I*. *I* is the subject pronoun (sp) because it tells who the second clause is about.

Object of the Preposition

Week 1 you learned that an **object of the preposition** is a noun or pronoun at the end of a prepositional phrase. **PATTERN preposition + noun (no verb)**

    To the frog begins with a preposition (to), ends with a noun (frog), and has no verb in between. The noun *frog* is the object of the preposition (op) because it is the noun at the end of the prepositional phrase.

Noun of Direct Address

Week 5 you learned that a **noun of direct address** is a noun used to directly address someone. It only appears in a quoted sentence.

    The noun *Frederick* is a noun of direct address (nda) because it is the noun the king uses to directly address the frog.

> An NDA is never the subject of the sentence. A noun can do only one job at a time.

The next two jobs are similar. Find both by asking *subject verb what?* or *subject verb whom?*

Direct Object

A **direct object** is a noun or pronoun that follows an action verb and answers the question *what* or *whom*. A direct object receives the verb's action. That means it completes the verb's meaning.

    King showed what? *hospitality*. The noun *hospitality* follows the action verb and functions as the direct object (do) because *hospitality* tells what the *king showed*.

> The noun (or pronoun) that follows an action verb is called a direct object.

Predicate Noun

A **predicate noun** is a noun or pronoun that follows a linking verb and answers the question *what* or *whom*. A predicate noun renames the subject. The subject and predicate noun are different names for the same person, place, thing, or idea.

    I am whom? *King Morton*. The noun *King Morton* follows the linking verb and functions as the predicate noun (pn) because *King Morton* is another name for *I*.

> The noun (or pronoun) that follows a linking verb is called a predicate noun.

Mark It!   Continue to mark every verb as *av*, *lv*, or *hv*.

    Mark every subject noun (*sn*), subject pronoun (*sp*), object of the preposition (*op*), noun of direct address (*nda*), direct object (*do*), predicate noun (*pn*), and appositive (*app*).

Who/Which Clause

Week 7 you learned that a **who/which clause** is a dependent clause that describes the noun it follows. A *who/which* clause is easy to recognize because it begins with the word *who* or *which*.

                            w/w
[King Morton ruled the land], (which was an obscure kingdom).

Invisible Who/Which Clause

An **invisible who/which clause** occurs when the *who* or *which* and the verb are removed from the clause. They become invisible.

                            w/w
[King Morton ruled the land], (~~which was~~ an obscure kingdom).

If a *who/which* clause contains a *be* verb, the *who* or *which* and the *be* verb can be removed to form an invisible *who/which* clause.

Be Verbs
   am, is, are, was, were, be, being, been

                     which was   app
[King Morton ruled the land], (an obscure kingdom).

In this example, the words *which was* are implied. They are not written in the sentence. When the words "which was" are removed, the words that remain are called an appositive phrase.

An **appositive** (app) is a noun or noun phrase that renames the noun it follows. The noun and the appositive are different names for the same person, place, thing, or idea. *Kingdom* is another name for *land*.

Phrase Overview: Appendix III

An appositive often includes words that describe it. In the example *kingdom* is the noun that functions as an appositive. *An obscure kingdom* is the appositive phrase.

Follow the same comma rules for the invisible *who/which* clause (the appositive phrase) that you follow for the regular *who/which* clause.

  , Place commas around a *who/which* clause if it is nonessential.

  ✗ Do not place commas around a *who/which* clause if it is essential (changes the meaning of the sentence).

Mark It! Mentally insert *who* or *which* and the *be* verb. Place parentheses around the invisible *who/which* clause. Write **app** above the appositive.

                    w/w   app
[I am King Morton], ((who is) ruler of this land).

Run-On

Fix It! no longer tells you how to fix the run-on sentence. You must determine yourself if a run-on exists and how to eliminate it. If the passage contains two or more main clauses in one sentence, look for a run-on.

Remember, there are three simple ways to fix a run-on:

- **.** Place a period at the end of each main clause. This is the simplest fix.

- **;** Fix It! will indicate if a semicolon is the best option.

- **, cc** If a coordinating conjunction (cc) connects two main clauses, confirm that a comma is in front of the cc. The cc without a comma is a comma error.

Read It!	Mark It!	Fix It!	Week 11
			Day 1
1 vocabulary	10 noun/pronoun jobs	1 indent	
	2 <u>prepositional phrases</u>	2 capitals	
	4 [main clauses]	5 commas	
	4 subject-verb pairs (s v)	2 end marks	
	1 opener	2 quotation marks	
		1 apostrophe	

hopping behind her the frog followed Dorinda, to the elaborate dining hall, I appreciate your hospitality **sire** Im Frederick the frog volunteered.

Rewrite It!

Read It!   **Mark It!**   **Fix It!**   Week 11

Day 2

1 vocabulary

8 noun/pronoun jobs
1 coordinating conjunction (cc)
1 prepositional phrase
4 [main clauses]
4 subject-verb pairs (s v)

2 indents
2 capitals
4 commas
2 end marks
6 quotation marks
1 apostrophe

Dorinda pick up Frederick her father commanded and feed him from your golden plate. yuck then I wont touch another bite she **whined**

Rewrite It! _____

_____
_____
_____
_____

Read It!	Mark It!	Fix It!	
			Week 11
			Day 3
1 vocabulary	11 noun/pronoun jobs	1 indent	
	1 coordinating conjunction (cc)	2 capitals	
	2 prepositional phrases	5 commas	
	2 [main clauses]	1 end mark	
	1 *who/which* clause (w/w)	2 quotation marks	
	1 *that* clause (that)		
	4 subject-verb pairs (s v)		
	1 invisible *who/which* clause (w/w)		
	2 openers		

patiently King Morton who valued **integrity** explained that "a promise was a promise," additionally he reminded Dorinda about her royal duties and the expectations of the people the nation's citizens.

Rewrite It!

Week 11
Day 4

Read It!

1 vocabulary

Mark It!

8 noun/pronoun jobs
1 coordinating conjunction (cc)
2 prepositional phrases
2 [main clauses]
1 adverb clause (AC)
3 subject-verb pairs (s v)
2 openers

Fix It!

1 indent
1 capital
4 commas
1 apostrophe

Dorinda **complied**, because she would not touch the frog, with her own precious finger's she held her napkin between her thumb, and first finger.

Rewrite It!

Learn It!

Pronoun

A **pronoun** takes the place of a noun. Without pronouns, a passage would sound monotonous, even strange. An **antecedent** is the word the pronoun refers to. If the antecedent is not mentioned or if it is unclear, confusion occurs.

> She laughed and yelled, "Give him that!"
>> Who is she? Who is him? What is that? These sentences are confusing because the pronouns are missing antecedents.

> Dorinda gave Maribella toast with sturgeon roe. She wrinkled her face.
>> Who wrinkled her face, Dorinda or Maribella? The antecedent is unclear.

Pronoun Case

Pronouns function like nouns. However, specific pronouns do only certain jobs.

Subjective case pronouns do the job of subject nouns and predicate nouns.

> *sn*　　　　　　　　　　*sp*
> Frederick knocked at the door. Who knocked at the door?
>> Who knocked? *Frederick, subject noun*
>> Who knocked? *Who, subject pronoun*

> *lv*　*pn*　　　　*lv*　*pn*
> The prince is a frog. The prince is he.
>> Prince is who? *frog* The noun *frog* follows the linking verb and renames the subject.
>> Prince is who? *he* The pronoun *he* follows the linking verb and renames the subject.

Objective case pronouns do the job of direct objects and objects of a preposition.

> *av*　　*do*　　　　　*av*　*do*
> The frog followed Dorinda. The frog followed her.
>> Followed whom? *Dorinda* The noun *Dorinda* follows the action verb.
>> Followed whom? *her* The pronoun *her* follows the action verb.

> 　　　　　*op*　　　　　　　*op*
> You will sit with the frog. I must sit with whom?
>> The noun *frog* follows the preposition.
>> The pronoun *whom* follows the preposition.

Possessive case pronouns do the job of adjectives and predicate nouns.

> 　　　　　*adj*　　　　　　　　　　*adj*
> The frog ate from Dorinda's plate. The frog ate from her plate.
>> From whose plate? *Dorinda's*
>> From whose plate? *her*

> 　　　　　　　　　*pn*　　　　　　　　*pn*
> The delicious dinner was Dorinda's food. The dinner was hers.
>> Was what? *food* The noun *food* follows the linking verb and renames the subject.
>> Was what? *hers* The pronoun *hers* follows the linking verb and renames the subject.

Week 12

8 Parts of Speech

Pronoun

Definition: A pronoun replaces a noun in order to avoid repetition.

List: Appendix III

Subjective Case
subject
predicate noun
I
you
he, she, it
we
you
they
who

Objective Case
direct object
object of preposition
me
you
him, her, it
us
you
them
whom

Possessive Case	
adjective	predicate pronoun
my	mine
your	yours
his, her, its	his, hers, its
our	ours
your	yours
their	theirs
whose	whose

Think About It!

Fill in the blanks with a word from the word bank. Use each word one time.

Word Bank
- he
- her
- his
- it
- its
- me
- mine
- theirs
- them
- they
- us
- we
- whom
- whose
- you
- you

Case	Subjective	Objective	Possessive	
Function (job)	subject / predicate pronoun	direct object / object of prep	adjective	predicate pronoun
	I		my	
	you		your	yours
	she	him	it	her	his	hers	its
			our	ours
		you	your	yours
			their	
	who			

What Is It and Why?

Read each sentence and determine if the underlined pronoun is a subjective case, an objective case, or a possessive case pronoun.

Write the type of pronoun in the blank and explain why.

Dorinda was bored. <u>She</u> and Maribella went to town.

subjective case Why? _**She** is the subject of the clause._

Dorinda spotted the frog, <u>who</u> sat near a store.

_____ Why? _____

"Oh no! It is <u>he</u>!"

_____ Why? _____

Maribella kindly greeted <u>him</u>.

_____ Why? _____

"Would you come into the store with <u>us</u>?"

_____ Why? _____

He saw the store. <u>Its</u> door was closed.

_____ Why? _____

Maribella started to open the door, but Frederick stopped <u>her</u>.

_____ Why? _____

Week 12

Day 1

Read It!	Mark It!	Fix It!
1 vocabulary	10 noun/pronoun jobs 1 coordinating conjunction (cc) 4 prepositional phrases 3 [main clauses] 3 subject-verb pairs (s v) 3 openers	4 commas 2 end marks 1 apostrophe

Unceremoniously, she grabbed one of Fredericks hind legs and deposited him on the table, beside her plate he was a revolting, green amphibian, promptly she receded into her chair.

Rewrite It! _____

Week 12

Day 2

Read It!	Mark It!	Fix It!
1 vocabulary	13 noun/pronoun jobs 2 <u>prepositional phrases</u> 4 [main clauses] 1 *who/which* clause (w/w) 1 *that* clause (that) 6 subject-verb pairs (s v) 3 openers	1 indent 2 capitals 5 commas 1 semicolon

After supper, King Morton invited Frederick, to the Guest Room which was a splendid suite. Velvet carpeted the floor, silk blanketed the bed. Frederick knew, that he would **relish** his palace stay.

Rewrite It! _____

Read It!	Mark It!	Fix It!	Week 12
1 vocabulary	7 noun/pronoun jobs	1 indent	Day 3
	2 coordinating conjunctions (cc)	5 commas	
	2 [main clauses]	1 end mark	
	2 subject-verb pairs (s v)		
	2 openers		

Evidently Dorinda Maribella and King Morton had not **deduced** the frog's true identity, Frederick was not a lowly frog, but a royal prince.

Rewrite It! _____

Week 12

Read It!	Mark It!	Fix It!	Day 4
1 vocabulary	11 noun/pronoun jobs	1 indent	
	5 <u>prepositional phrases</u>	2 capitals	
	2 [main clauses]	6 commas	
	1 adverb clause (AC)	1 end mark	
	3 subject-verb pairs (s v)	1 apostrophe	
	1 invisible *who/which* clause (w/w)		
	2 openers		

When he had lived at his fathers castle Frederick had been a swollen-headed **pretentious** teenager on a humid afternoon in July young Frederick had been riding his horse a strong thoroughbred through a forest in his father's, vast Kingdom.

Rewrite It! _____

_____
_____
_____
_____

Learn It!

Pronoun Types

There are more than one hundred pronouns in the English language. Grammarians organize pronouns in various ways. One way to organize pronouns is by type.

Some pronouns appear in more than one category. For example, when *who* begins a dependent clause (a *who/which* clause) it is classified as a relative pronoun. When *who* begins a question, it is classified as an interrogative pronoun.

A **personal pronoun** refers to a specific person, place, or thing recently mentioned. In English there are three persons: first, second, and third.

> The chef had served a new dessert. Dorinda looked at Maribella.
>
> "I see that *you* did not eat the ice cream that *she* made."
>
>> The antecedent for *I*, the first-person pronoun, is Dorinda, the person speaking.
>>
>> The antecedent for *you*, the second-person pronoun, is Maribella, the person spoken to.
>>
>> The antecedent for *she*, the third-person pronoun, is the chef, the person spoken about.

Personal

1st
I, me, my, mine, we, us, our, ours

2nd
you, your, yours

3rd
he, him, his, she, her, hers, it, its, they, them, their, theirs

A **reflexive pronoun** ends in *-self* or *-selves*, functions as an object, and reflects the subject of the same clause.

> The king mumbled to *himself*.
>
>> The pronoun *himself* is the object of the preposition *to* and reflects (refers to) the subject of the clause. The antecedent for the pronoun *himself* is the subject of the clause, the noun *king*.

An **intensive pronoun** ends in *-self* or *-selves*, functions as an appositive, and intensifies the noun or pronoun it refers to. Intensive pronouns can be removed from the sentence.

> The frog *himself* spoke to the king.
>
>> The pronoun *himself* emphasizes the noun *frog*. The antecedent for the pronoun *himself* is the noun *frog*, and the intensive pronoun can be removed from the sentence: *The frog spoke to the king*.

Reflexive and Intensive

same words, different uses

myself, yourself, himself, herself, itself, ourselves, yourselves, themselves

A **relative pronoun** begins a dependent adjective clause (a *who/which* clause) and refers to the noun the entire clause describes.

> The frog, *who* used to be a prince, spoke respectfully yet boldly.
>
>> The *who* clause describes *frog*, the noun it follows. The antecedent for the pronoun *who* is the noun *frog*. *The frog used to be a prince*.
>
> The king, *whom* the frog addressed, listened intently.
>
>> The *who* clause describes *king*, the noun it follows. The antecedent for the pronoun *whom* is the noun *king*. *The frog addressed the king*.

Relative

who, whom, whose, which, that

An **interrogative pronoun** begins a question. The antecedent is the answer to the question.

> *What* was the frog's name?
>
>> The pronoun *what* begins a question. The antecedent for the pronoun *what* is the answer to the question: *Frederick was the frog's name*.

Interrogative

what, whatever, which, whichever, who, whoever, whom, whose

Demonstrative
this, that, these, those

A **demonstrative pronoun** points to a particular person or thing. *This* and *that* refer to singular items. *These* and *those* refer to plural items.

> *This* was an unusual frog.

The antecedent for the pronoun *this* is the noun *frog*.

Indefinite
all, another, any, anybody, anyone, anything, anywhere, both, each, either, everybody, everyone, everything, everywhere, few, more, most, much, neither, no one, nobody, none, nothing, nowhere, one, other, others, own, several, some, somebody, someone, something, somewhere

An **indefinite pronoun** is not specific. Indefinite pronouns do not refer to a particular person, place, or thing and will not have a defined antecedent.

> *Everything* on the table smelled good.

The reader can only assume it was food that smelled good because the pronoun *everything* does not have an antecedent.

Mark It! Continue to mark every verb as *av*, *lv*, or *hv*.

Continue to mark every subject noun (*sn*), subject pronoun (*sp*), object of the preposition (*op*), noun of direct address (*nda*), direct object (*do*), predicate noun (*pn*), and appositive (*app*).

Think About It!

Demonstrative pronouns, indefinite pronouns, and possessive case pronouns function as adjectives when they come before a noun.

> This was an unusual amphibian. This frog spoke.

In the first sentence *This* is a demonstrative pronoun and functions as the subject of the clause. The antecedent of the pronoun *this* is *frog*.

In the second sentence *This* comes before the noun *frog* and tells which frog. It functions as an adjective.

Reflexive pronouns and objective case pronouns function as objects. When the object refers to the subject of the clause, a reflexive pronoun is used. Think of the *reflexive* pronoun as a pronoun *reflecting* its subject.

> First Dorinda served herself. Then Dorinda served her.

In the first sentence the direct object *herself* refers to the subject *Dorinda*. *Herself* is a reflexive pronoun reflecting its subject.

In the second sentence Dorinda served another girl. We know this because the direct object is the objective case pronoun *her*.

Reflexive pronouns and intensive pronouns are the same pronouns with different uses. A reflexive pronoun functions as an object and is a necessary part of the sentence. An intensive pronoun functions as an appositive to show emphasis and can be removed from the sentence.

> The frog thought to himself about how Dorinda herself might help him.

Himself is a reflexive pronoun because it is the object of the preposition *to* and refers to (reflects) the subject *frog*. It is a necessary part of the sentence because without it, *to* would not have an object.

Herself is an intensive pronoun because it is an appositive that emphasizes *Dorinda*, the noun it follows.

Read It!	Mark It!	Fix It!	Week 13 Day 1
1 vocabulary	12 noun/pronoun jobs 3 <u>prepositional phrases</u> 4 [main clauses] 2 adverb clauses (AC) 6 subject-verb pairs (s v) 1 opener	1 indent 3 capitals 7 commas 2 end marks 4 quotation marks 1 apostrophe	

After he had ridden for several miles his horse reared up, because a thin, young boy stood in the path. please Sir Ive lost my way the boy explained, can I have a ride out of this **daunting** forest

Rewrite It!

Week 13
Day 2

Read It!	Mark It!	Fix It!
1 vocabulary	7 noun/pronoun jobs	1 indent
	2 prepositional phrases	2 capitals
	3 [main clauses]	4 commas
	1 *that* clause (that)	1 end mark
	4 subject-verb pairs (s v)	4 quotation marks
	1 opener	

Get out of my way Peasant the rude thoughtless prince retorted he was **oblivious**, that the boy was a "wizard" in disguise.

Rewrite It! _____

Read It!	**Mark It!**	**Fix It!**	Week 13
1 vocabulary	8 noun/pronoun jobs	1 indent	Day 3
	1 coordinating conjunction (cc)	2 capitals	
	3 <u>prepositional phrases</u>	3 commas	
	2 [main clauses]	1 end mark	
	2 subject-verb pairs (s v)	2 quotation marks	
	1 invisible *who/which* clause (w/w)	2 apostrophes	
	1 opener		

instantly the boys voice thundered for your lack of compassion and **decency** you must spend your day's as a frog a worthless creature

Rewrite It!

Week 13

Day 4

Read It!	**Mark It!**	**Fix It!**
1 vocabulary	6 noun/pronoun jobs	1 capital
	2 coordinating conjunctions (cc)	4 commas
	2 <u>prepositional phrases</u>	1 end mark
	2 [main clauses]
	2 subject-verb pairs (s v)
	1 opener

Staring reproachfully the boy zapped the air and the Prince found himself hopping off the saddle, and **plummeting**, to the ground

Rewrite It!

Learn It!

Week 14

Usage Errors
You no longer need to label verb types or noun and pronoun functions. However, from now on you must identify and fix common usage errors. These errors will include homophones, subject-verb agreement, verb tense, and pronouns.

Fix It!   Place a line through the incorrect word and write the correct word above it.

Frederick loved horses. One year his father had given his brother
and ~~he~~ *him* beautiful stallions. Prince Frederick ~~spends~~ *spent* many hours
cleaning and brushing ~~there~~ *their* horses so that they could ride
through the countryside.

Invisible Prepositions
A **prepositional phrase** begins with a preposition and ends with a noun or pronoun, which is called the object of the preposition. When a prepositional phrase begins a sentence, label it as a #2 sentence opener.

Pattern:
preposition + noun
(no verb)

Maribella hosted a dinner ~~on~~ Monday.

She celebrated her birthday ~~on~~ the first of April.
> The preposition *on* can be dropped when the prepositional phrase refers to time. In the sentence *Maribella hosted a dinner Monday*, the preposition *on* is implied, not written. *Monday* is the object of the unwritten or invisible preposition.

Maribella hosted a dinner ~~on~~ last Monday.

Maribella will host a book club ~~on~~ next week.
> Prepositions of time are always dropped before the adjectives *last, next, this, that, some, every*. The phrase ends with a noun. The words between the unwritten or invisible preposition and the noun are adjectives, never verbs.

Invisible #2 Prepositional Opener
An **invisible #2 prepositional opener** is formed when a word or phrase indicating time is followed by a main clause. The preposition *on* or *during* is implied.

② prepositional

Pattern:
preposition + noun
(no verb)

②
(during) That afternoon [Dorinda went shopping].
> The preposition *during* is implied. You can confirm that this is a prepositional opener by inserting a preposition and making sure the phrase follows the PATTERN preposition + noun (no verb).

comma if 5+ words

Mark It!   Underline the invisible prepositional phrase and write **on** or **during** where the preposition could be inserted.

②
(on) Last Friday [she bought a diamond tiara].

Dependent Clause

That **Clause**

Pattern:
that + subject + verb

First Word:
that
(may be invisible)

Commas:
none

Marking:
that

Invisible *That* Clause

An **invisible *that* clause** occurs when the word *that* is implied, not stated directly. The word *that* is invisible.

    s   v   s   v   v
Frederick knew a royal kiss could restore him.
This sentence has two subject-verb pairs and appears to have two main clauses.

    s   v   s   v   v
Frederick knew. A royal kiss could restore him.
If you insert a period, the sentences do not make sense. A main clause must express a complete thought. What did Frederick know? These words must be in the same sentence in order to make sense.

    s   v   *that*   s   v   v
[Frederick knew] (a royal kiss could restore him).
The word *that* is implied, not written in the sentence. The second clause is a dependent *that* clause. You can confirm this by inserting the word *that* into the sentence: Frederick knew (that) a royal kiss could restore him.

Mark It! Place parentheses around the invisible *that* clause and write ***that*** where the word *that* could be inserted. Write ***v*** above each verb and ***s*** above each subject.

    s   v   *that*   s   v   v
He realized ((*that*) he must befriend a princess).

Number Words/Numerals

Use words for numbers expressed in one or two words and ordinal numbers.

    twenty   fifty-three   three hundred
    first   second   third

Use numerals for numbers that use three or more words, for numbers mixed with symbols, and for dates.

    123   204
    $500   40%
    December 25, not December 25th

Week 14

Read It!	Mark It!	Fix It!	Day 1

1 vocabulary

1 coordinating conjunction (cc)
4 prepositional phrases
3 [main clauses]
1 *who/which* clause (w/w)
1 adverb clause (AC)
5 subject-verb pairs (s v)
1 opener

2 capitals
6 commas
1 end mark
1 quotation mark
1 usage

The wizard continued as a frog, you might learn **humility**, and gratitude for simple kindnesses, which people offer yourself, you will be restored to normal, if a princess kisses you in true kindheartedness.

No closing quotation mark because quote continues.

Rewrite It!

Week 14

Day 2

Read It!	Mark It!	Fix It!
1 vocabulary	3 prepositional phrases	1 indent
	2 [main clauses]	5 commas
	2 *that* clauses (that)	1 quotation mark
	1 adverb clause (AC)	1 number
	5 subject-verb pairs (s v)	1 usage
	1 opener	

No opening quotation mark because quote continues.

If you ever confess, that you are a prince you will be **fated** to froghood forever. The frog had kept his secret for 6, long years hoping, he would eventually return too normal.

Rewrite It! _____

_____

_____

_____

82 Institute for Excellence in Writing *Fix It! Grammar: Frog Prince* Student Book Level 5

Read It!	Mark It!	Fix It!	Week 14
			Day 3
1 vocabulary	1 coordinating conjunction (cc)	4 commas	
	4 <u>prepositional phrases</u>	1 end mark	
	2 [main clauses]	1 apostrophe	
	1 *who/which* clause (w/w)		
	1 *that* clause (that)		
	4 subject-verb pairs (s v)		
	1 opener		

Frederick had resided as a frog in King Mortons **sequestered** expansive garden and he had wished, one of the princesses who frequently spent time in the garden would be his friend

Rewrite It!

Week 14

Day 4

Read It!	Mark It!	Fix It!
1 vocabulary	1 coordinating conjunction (cc)	1 indent
	2 <u>prepositional phrases</u>	1 capital
	2 [main clauses]	6 commas
	1 adverb clause (AC)	1 end mark
	3 subject-verb pairs (s v)	
	1 invisible *who/which* clause (w/w)	
	2 openers	

Unfortunately for him he had met Dorinda, before he had met Maribella, that evening, he assessed the situation, and **conjectured** how to charm Dorinda the younger princess.

Rewrite It! _____

Learn It!

Adjective

An **adjective** describes a noun or pronoun. An adjectives tells which one, what kind, how many, or whose.

Adjectives come in three forms.

Single Word Adjectives

An adjective can come before the noun it describes, or it can follow a linking verb and describe the subject of the clause.

    adj   *adj*
The green frog croaked. The frog was green.

The adjective *green* describes *frog*. Which frog? *green*

Phrasal Adjectives

A **prepositional phrase** begins with a preposition and ends with a noun or pronoun. The entire phrase functions as a single unit. That means while each word in the prepositional phrase has its own job, all the words work together to do the job of an adjective or an adverb.

If a prepositional phrase comes immediately after a noun and describes that noun, the entire phrase does the job of an adjective.

      pp adj
The frog with green skin croaked.

With green skin is a prepositional phrase. The entire phrase is a phrasal adjective that comes after a noun and describes that noun. Which frog? *with green skin*

A **participial phrase** begins with a present participle, an -ing word. The entire phrase describes a noun in the sentence and does the job of an adjective.

-ing adj
Wearing a top hat, the frog croaked.

      -ing adj
The frog, wearing a top hat, croaked.

Wearing a top hat is a participial (-ing) phrase. The entire phrase is a phrasal adjective that describes a noun in the sentence. Which frog? *wearing a top hat*

Clausal Adjectives

A *who/which* clause is a dependent clause that begins with *who* or *which* and includes a subject and verb. The entire clause describes the noun it follows and does the job of an adjective.

    w/w
The frog, (who wore a top hat), croaked.

Who wore a top hat is a *who/which* clause. The entire clause is a clausal adjective that describes the noun it follows. Which frog? *who wore a top hat*

Mark It!   Weeks 15–16 write ***adj*** above each single word adjective.

              Write ***pp adj*** above each prepositional phrase that functions as an adjective.

              Write ***-ing adj*** above each participial phrase.

---

8 Parts of Speech

Adjective
Definition:
An adjective describes a noun or pronoun.

Test:
the ____ pen

Questions:
which one?
what kind?
how many?
whose?

prepositional phrase
    adjective or adverb
    adjective if it describes the noun it follows

participial -ing phrase
    adjective
    describes a noun in the sentence

who/which clause
    adjective
    describes the noun it follows

8 Parts of Speech

Adverb
Definition:
An adverb modifies a verb, an adjective, or another adverb.

Questions:
how?
when?
where?
why?
to what extent?

Adverb
An **adverb** modifies a verb, an adjective, or another adverb. An adverb tells how, when, where, why, to what extent.

Adverbs come in three forms.

Single Word Adverbs
An adverb often ends in -ly. However, many adverbs do not.

adv   *adv*

The frog usually croaked. The frog often croaked.

    The adverb *usually* modifies *croaked*. Croaked when? *usually*
    The adverb *often* modifies *croaked*. Croaked when? *often*

adv

The frog did not croak.

    The words *yes, no, not, too, even, else* function as adverbs.

Phrasal Adverbs
A **prepositional phrase** begins with a preposition and ends with a noun. The entire phrase functions as a single unit. That means while each word in the prepositional phrase has its own job, all the words work together to do the job of an adjective or an adverb.

If a prepositional phrase tells how, when, where, or why, the entire phrase does the job of an adverb.

<u>*pp adv*</u>

<u>In the morning</u> the frog croaked.

    In the morning is a prepositional phrase. The entire phrase is a phrasal adverb that modifies a verb in the sentence. Croaked when? *in the morning*

Clausal Adverbs
An **adverb clause** is a dependent clause that begins with a www word and includes a subject and verb. The entire clause modifies a verb in the sentence and does the job of an adverb.

AC

The frog croaked **(**as he woke**)**.

    As he woke is an adverb clause. The entire clause is a clausal adverb that modifies a verb in the sentence. Croaked when? *as he woke*

Mark It!   Weeks 15–16 write ***adv*** above each single word adverb.
                Write <u>***pp adv***</u> above each prepositional phrase that functions as an adverb.

Quality Adjectives and -ly Adverbs
Like strong verbs, quality adjectives and -ly adverbs create a strong image or feeling. Continue to look for quality adjectives and -ly adverbs in this book and write them on the collection pages in Appendix II. Use these words in your own writing.

Week 15

Day 1

Read It!

1 vocabulary

Mark It!

3 adjectives (adj)
2 adverbs (adv)
1 coordinating conjunction (cc)
5 prep phrases (pp adj) or (pp adv)
1 [main clause]
1 who/which clause (w/w)
1 that clause (that)
3 subject-verb pairs (s v)
1 opener

Fix It!

1 indent
6 commas
1 usage

The next morning during a **substantial** breakfast of omelets pastries and fruit King Morton who always treats his guests with generosity graciously insisted, that Frederick stay for a week.

Rewrite It!

Week 15

Read It!   **Mark It!**   **Fix It!**   Day 2

1 vocabulary

4 adjectives (adj)
3 adverbs (adv)
1 coordinating conjunction (cc)
2 prep phrases (pp adj) or (pp adv)
1 -ing phrase (-ing adj)
3 [main clauses]
1 *that* clause (that)
1 adverb clause (AC)
5 subject-verb pairs (s v)
2 openers

1 indent
1 capital
3 commas
2 end marks
2 quotation marks
1 apostrophe

Dorinda groaned. Glancing down she noticed that Fredericks hind leg was **inadvertently** touching her omelet ew she cried, as she swept him from her plate, and spitefully hurled him against the wall.

Rewrite It! _____

88   Institute for Excellence in Writing *Fix It! Grammar: Frog Prince* Student Book Level 5

Week 15

Day 3

Read It!	Mark It!	Fix It!
1 vocabulary	5 adjectives (adj)	2 indents
	1 adverb (adv)	4 commas
	2 <u>prep phrases</u> (<u>pp adj</u>) or (<u>pp adv</u>)	4 end marks
	1 -ing phrase (-ing adj)	6 quotation marks
	5 [main clauses]	1 apostrophe
	2 *that* clauses (that)	
	7 subject-verb pairs (s v)	
	1 opener	

Ow he grunted I believe my leg is broken Dorinda **feigned** remorse, for her unkind action's mumbling an apology I wish I had broken all, of your legs she muttered pitilessly.

Rewrite It! _____

Week 15
Day 4

Read It!	Mark It!	Fix It!
1 vocabulary	3 adjectives (adj)	1 indent
	1 adverb (adv)	4 commas
	1 coordinating conjunction (cc)	1 end mark
	3 prep phrases (pp adj) or (pp adv)	1 apostrophe
	1 -ing phrase (-ing adj)	1 usage
	3 [main clauses]	
	3 subject-verb pairs (s v)	
	3 openers	

Dorindas behavior **mortifies** her father, King Morton gently lifted the frog placed him on a silver tray and carried him to the doctor, caring for the animals. He ordered Dorinda to follow.

Rewrite It!

Learn It!

Clausal Adjectives and Clausal Adverbs
In this book you have looked at the first word of a dependent clause to determine if the dependent clause functions as an adjective or as an adverb.

> If a dependent clause begins with a www word, it usually functions as an adverb.
> > Adverb clauses can appear anywhere in a sentence.
> > Use a comma after, not before, an adverb clause.
> If a dependent clause begins with *who* or *which*, it functions as an adjective.
> > A *who/which* clause follows a noun and describes it.
> > Use commas unless essential.

Although the words *when* and *where* are www words, these two words can also begin adjective clauses.
> To determine if a dependent clause that begins with *when* or *where* is an adjective clause or an adverb clause, look at its location. If it comes immediately after a noun and describes that noun, it is an adjective clause.
> You can test if a dependent clause that begins with *when* or *where* is an adjective clause by inserting *which was* or *which were* before the clause.

> Frederick remained in the infirmary, *(which was)* where he rested).
> > *Where he rested* is a dependent clause. It begins with the word *where* and includes a subject and a verb.
> > The dependent clause follows the noun *infirmary* and describes it. Which infirmary? *where he rested* It makes sense to say *Frederick remained in the infirmary (which was) where he rested*, so this is an adjective clause.
> > It is a nonessential because without the clause, Frederick still remained in the infirmary. It requires a comma.

> **,** Place commas around an adjective clause if it is nonessential.
> **✗** Do not place commas around an adjective clause if it is essential (changes the meaning of the sentence).

Mark It! Place parentheses around the dependent clause (DC).
Write *v* above each verb and *s* above each subject.
If the dependent clause (DC) begins with *when* or *where*, decide if it is an adjective clause or an adverb clause.
If it is an adjective clause, the test (who was/were or which was/were) works.
If it is an adverb clause, write *AC* above the www word.
Follow the comma rules.

 s v
The vet worked during the day, (*(which was)* when Frederick was awake).

 AC   s   v
Dorinda would apologize, (when she felt like it).

Adverb Clause
Pattern:
www word + subject + verb

First Word:
> when, while, where, as, since, if, although, because, after, before, until, unless, whenever, whereas, than

Commas:
after, not before

Marking:
AC

Adjective Clause
Location:
describes the noun it follows

First Word:
> who, whom, whose, which, when, where, that

Commas:
unless essential

Marking:
w/w if it begins with *who* or *which*

That Clause

A *that* clause can be an adjective clause or a noun clause. While each word in the *that* clause has its own job, all the words work together to do the job of either a noun or an adjective. In this book, most *that* clauses are noun clauses that function as direct objects.

To determine if a *that* clause functions as an adjective or as a noun, look at its location. If it comes immediately after a noun and describes that noun, it is an adjective clause.

You can test if a *that* clause is an adjective clause by replacing *that* with *which*.

which
The leg (~~that~~ was broken) had to be set.

The *that* clause follows the noun *leg* and describes it. Which leg? *that was broken*

It makes sense to say *The leg ~~that~~ which was broken had to be set.* This *that* clause is an adjective clause.

Frederick knew (that his leg was broken).

Frederick knew what? *that his leg was broken* This *that* clause is a noun clause that follows the action verb and functions as the direct object.

That clauses that function like nouns and *that* clauses that function like adjectives are essential to the sentence.

✗ *That* clauses do not take commas.

Think About It!

Both adjectives and adverbs add detail to a sentence. When a prepositional phrase or a dependent clause tells how, when, where, or why, the entire word group does the job of an adverb. When a prepositional phrase or a dependent clause comes after a noun and describes the noun, the entire word group does the job of an adjective and tells which one, what kind, how many, or whose.

These two sentences contain similar words but have different meanings.

The veterinarian examined Frederick <u>in the infirmary</u>.

Examined where? *in the infirmary*

In the infirmary comes after the noun *Frederick*, but it does not describe *Frederick*. It is not an adjective.

In the infirmary tells where the veterinarian examined Frederick, so it is an adverb.

The veterinarian <u>from the infirmary</u> examined Frederick.

Which veterinarian? *from the infirmary*

From the infirmary comes after the noun *veterinarian* and describes it.

From the infirmary tells which veterinarian examined Frederick, so it is an adjective.

Strong Verb, Quality Adjective, and -ly Adverb

A strong verb, a quality adjective, and an -ly adverb are three different ways to dress up writing. These stylistic devices create a strong image and feeling. A strong verb is an action verb, never a linking or helping verb. A quality adjective is more specific than a weak adjective. A weak adjective is overused, boring, or vague. An -ly adverb is used to enhance the meaning of the verb, adjective, or adverb that it modifies.

Continue to look for strong verbs, quality adjectives, and -ly adverbs in this book and write them on the collection pages found in Appendix II.

Week 16
Day 1

Read It!

1 vocabulary

Mark It!

7 adjectives (adj)
1 adverb (adv)
2 prep phrases (pp adj) or (pp adv)
2 [main clauses]
1 who/which clause (w/w)
1 adverb clause (AC)
5 subject-verb pairs (s v)
2 openers

Fix It!

1 indent
1 capital
4 commas
1 end mark

In the infirmary the palace vet positioned the frog on the adjustable, exam table where he treated his smallest patients after he examined Frederick he set the broken frog leg which **dangled** oddly.

Rewrite It!

Read It!	Mark It!	Fix It!	Week 16
			Day 2
1 vocabulary	1 adjective (adj)	1 indent	
	1 adverb (adv)	1 capital	
	2 coordinating conjunctions (cc)	6 commas	
	2 prep phrases (pp adj) or (pp adv)	2 end marks	
	4 [main clauses]	4 quotation marks	
	1 *who/which* clause (w/w)	1 apostrophe	
	5 subject-verb pairs (s v)		

Frogs are animal's, which heal slowly so it will be a lengthy **convalescence** the vet informed King Morton, and Dorinda, he will stay in the infirmary, for a month

Rewrite It!

Read It!	Mark It!	Fix It!	Week 16
1 vocabulary	4 adjectives (adj)	1 indent	Day 3
	1 -ing phrase (-ing adj)	4 commas	
	2 [main clauses]	3 apostrophes	
	1 *that* clause (that)		
	1 adverb clause (AC)		
	5 subject-verb pairs (s v)		
	2 openers		

Hearing the doctors announcement Dorinda became **sullen**. After her father insisted, that she deliver Fredericks meal's she regretted the day, when the accident happened.

Rewrite It!

Week 16

Day 4

Read It!

1 vocabulary

Mark It!

1 adjective (adj)
1 adverb (adv)
2 [main clauses]
1 *that* clause (that)
2 adverb clauses (AC)
6 subject-verb pairs (s v)
2 openers

Fix It!

1 capital
3 commas
1 end mark

Dorinda **resolved** to avoid the infirmary where Frederick now stayed, when the king ordered her to assist Frederick while he recuperated she knew it would be difficult.

Rewrite It!

Review It!

Week 17

Clausal Adverb or Clausal Adjective?

The words *when*, *where*, and *that* begin different types of dependent clauses.
If *when* or *where* begins an adverb clause, use a comma after, not before. AC, MC MC AC
If *when* or *where* begins an adjective clause, use commas unless essential.
That clauses are always essential and never use commas.

   Read each sentence, underline the dependent clause, and identify it.
   For adjective clauses, circle the noun that the clause describes. Punctuate correctly.

The king told Dorinda to read stories that she loved to Frederick.
   adverb   **nonessential adjective**   **essential adjective**

Look at location.

The morning when the king issued his command was damp and cold.
   adverb   **nonessential adjective**   **essential adjective**

If the dependent clause comes immediately after a noun and describes that noun, it is an adjective clause.

Frederick was concerned when Dorinda took him from the infirmary.
   adverb   **nonessential adjective**   **essential adjective**

Adverb Clause
use comma after, not before
AC, MC   ,
MC AC   ✗

Dorinda knew to take him where her father had told her.
   adverb   **nonessential adjective**   **essential adjective**

They went to the palace library where the imperial collection was kept.
   adverb   **nonessential adjective**   **essential adjective**

Nonessential Adjective Clause
adds information to the sentence
use commas   ,

Frederick grimaced when she selected *How to Rid Your Garden of Pests*.
   adverb   **nonessential adjective**   **essential adjective**

He suggested books that told engaging stories instead.
   adverb   **nonessential adjective**   **essential adjective**

Essential Adjective Clause
defines the noun it follows
do not use commas   ✗

She found *Frog and Toad Are Friends* where the children's books were.
   adverb   **nonessential adjective**   **essential adjective**

Frederick noticed *The Frog Prince* on the shelf where fairytales resided.
   adverb   **nonessential adjective**   **essential adjective**

***That* Clause**
always essential
do not take commas   ✗

Dorinda read her favorite part where the frog becomes a prince.
   adverb   **nonessential adjective**   **essential adjective**

Direct Quote

A **direct quote** is an exact copy of another person's written or spoken words.

Copy the original source exactly, including capitalization, spelling, and punctuation. If you need to change part of the sentence to make it grammatical, put the changed part in square brackets. Begin and end the the direct quote with quotation marks.

"[The princess] had a golden ball in her hand, which was her favourite play-thing, and she amused herself with tossing it into the air and catching it again as it fell."

The square brackets alert the reader that *The princess* was not used in the original. However, the meaning remains the same.

Although the word *favourite* is spelled differently in modern American English, the quote must be an exact copy of the original.

The Frog-Prince
by Edgar Taylor

ONE fine evening a young princess went into a wood, and sat down by the side of a cool spring of water. She had a golden ball in her hand, which was her favourite play-thing, and she amused herself with tossing it into the air and catching it again as it fell. After a time she threw it up so high that when she stretched out her hand to catch it, the ball bounded away and rolled along upon the ground, till at last it fell into the spring. The princess looked into the spring after her ball; but it was very deep, so deep that she could not see the bottom of it. Then she began to lament her loss, and said, "Alas! if I could only get my ball again, I would give all my fine clothes and jewels, and every thing

1

This *Fix It! Grammar* book is an adaptation of a story first recorded by the German brothers Jacob and Wilhelm Grimm. When Edgar Taylor translated the fairy tale into English, he changed the title to "The Frog-Prince" and altered the ending.

Read It!	Mark It!	Fix It!	Week 17
1 vocabulary	2 coordinating conjunctions (cc)	1 indent	Day 1
	2 prepositional phrases	1 capital	
	4 [main clauses]	6 commas	
	1 *that* clause (that)	4 quotation marks	
	5 subject-verb pairs (s v)	1 usage	
	1 opener		

She knew, that she would have to treat him royally but she could be a "royal pain." Dorinda read to Frederick you're favorite stories, in the **imperial** library the King announced, and walked away.

Rewrite It!

Week 17
Day 2

Read It!

1 vocabulary

Mark It!

6 prepositional phrases
2 [main clauses]
1 *that* clause (that)
1 adverb clause (AC)
4 subject-verb pairs (s v)
2 openers

Fix It!

1 indent
1 capital
5 commas
1 end mark
1 apostrophe
1 number
1 usage

Every day, Dorinda took Frederick to the library, whenever she entered the frog **marveled** at the 100's of colorful books, that covered the walls, from floor to ceiling.

Rewrite It!

Read It!	Mark It!	Fix It!	Week 17
1 vocabulary	1 coordinating conjunction (cc)	1 indent	Day 3
	5 prepositional phrases	1 capital	
	5 [main clauses]	4 commas	
	1 adverb clause (AC)	4 end marks	
	6 subject-verb pairs (s v)	4 quotation marks	
	1 opener	2 apostrophes	
		1 usage	

At last, Frederick has an idea lets play a game he eagerly **proffered**, as he searched the row in front of him, Ill read the first line of a story and you tell me the name of the book

Rewrite It!

Week 17

Day 4

Read It!	Mark It!	Fix It!
1 vocabulary	5 prepositional phrases	1 indent
	4 [main clauses]	1 capital
	1 *who/which* clause (w/w)	5 commas
	5 subject-verb pairs (s v)	1 end mark
	2 openers	1 usage

Agreeing **hesitantly** Dorinda sat beside Frederick who's scrawny, skeletal fingers opened a book in the light of the moon a little egg lay on a leaf read Frederick. Dorinda thought, for a moment.

Rewrite It!

Learn It!

Fix It!
Starting this week, the Fix It! section no longer indicates how many indents, commas, capitals, and end marks are needed in each passage. Make needed fixes based on grammar and punctuation rules. This is what you must do with your own writing too since no one tells you how many indents, commas, capitals, and end marks you need in the paragraphs that you write.

#4 -ing Opener Impostor
Week 5 you learned that a **#4 -ing opener** is a sentence that begins with a participial phrase. However, not every sentence that begins with a word that ends with the letters *ing* is a #4 -ing opener. You must consider what the words are doing in the sentence.

④ -ing   s   v

Guessing the title, [Dorinda enjoyed the game].

    When a participial phrase (#4 -ing opener) begins a sentence,
        a comma separates the -ing opener from the main clause, and
        the thing after the comma must be the thing doing the inging.

    When an -ing word functions as an adjective, it is called a participle. *Guessing the title* is a participial phrase because it functions as an adjective that describes the subject of the main clause (Dorinda).

① subject
     s   v

[Guessing the title entertained Dorinda].

    Guessing is the subject of the sentence. What entertained? *Guessing* (subject noun)

    When an -ing word functions as a noun, it is called a gerund. Mark it as a #1 subject opener.

② prepositional
     s   v

During the game [Dorinda laughed].

    During is a preposition, not a participle.

    If a sentence begins with the preposition *concerning, according to, regarding*, or *during*, mark it as a #2 prepositional opener.

Literary Titles
Capitalize the first word and the last word of titles and subtitles. Capitalize all other words except articles, coordinating conjunctions, and prepositions.

Dorinda read *Frog and Toad Are Friends* by Arnold Lobel.

    Italicize titles of full-length works: book, magazine, movie, newspaper, website.
    If handwriting, underline because you cannot italicize.

She recited the nursery rhyme "Five Little Speckled Frogs."

    Place titles found within a larger source in quotation marks: article, chapter, short story, poem, speech, webpage.

    Place commas and periods inside closing quotation marks.

The Word *That*

Although the word *that* usually begins a dependent *that* clause, it does not when the word *that* is a demonstrative pronoun or an adjective.

Demonstrative
this, that, these, those

Demonstrative Pronoun

A **pronoun** takes the place of a noun.

      s   op

That was the best book. I will read more about that.

Like other pronouns, demonstrative pronouns perform a noun function. In the first example, *that* is the subject of the main clause. In the second example, *that* is the object of the preposition *about*.

Adjective Questions
which one, what kind, how many, whose

Adjective

An **adjective** describes a noun or a pronoun. When a demonstrative pronoun comes before a noun, it functions as an adjective.

    adj   *adj*

That book was the best book. I will read more about that frog.

That comes before a noun and answers the question which one.
Which book? *that* Which frog? *that*

Confirm that the word *that* functions as an adjective by replacing *that* with *the*:
~~That~~ The book was the best book. I will read more about ~~that~~ the frog.

***That* Clause Pattern**
that + subject + verb

Dependent Clause

A **dependent clause** contains a subject and a verb but does not express a complete thought. A ***that* clause** is a dependent clause that begins with the word *that*.

                                               that   s   v

Dorinda did not recognize the sentence (that he read).

To confirm that the word *that* begins a *that* clause, look for a subject (he) and a verb (read).

When the word *that* begins a *that* clause, you can often remove it from the sentence:
Dorinda did not recognize the sentence ~~that~~ he read.

If the *that* clause is an adjective clause, you can replace the word *that* with *which*:
Dorinda did not recognize the sentence ~~that~~ which he read.

What Is It and Why?

Read each sentence and determine if the word *that* begins a dependent *that* clause or if it is a demonstrative pronoun or an adjective.

The library housed stacks of books that generations had enjoyed.

Dorinda had spent hours in that place.

She knew that she could always find a thrilling book.

Pointing to a book, Frederick said, "Can you reach that for me?"

Read It!	Mark It!	Fix It!	Week 18
			Day 1
1 vocabulary	1 <u>prepositional phrase</u>	? indents	
	3 [main clauses]	? capitals	
	1 adverb clause (AC)	? commas	
	4 subject-verb pairs (s v)	? end marks	
	1 invisible *who/which* clause (w/w)	2 quotation marks	
	1 opener		

That has to be The very hungry Caterpillar she **responded**, she had enjoyed that book a favorite of hers since she was a young child.

Rewrite It!

Read It!	Mark It!	Fix It!	Week 18
1 vocabulary	1 coordinating conjunction (cc) 6 [main clauses] 6 subject-verb pairs (s v) 2 openers	? indents ? capitals ? commas ? end marks 4 quotation marks 1 usage	Day 2

Playing the game improved her mood. Let me do one she said. There was a boy called Eustace Clarence Scrubb and he almost deserved it, hoping to **stump** Frederick she smirks.

Rewrite It!

Week 18
Day 3

Read It!	Mark It!	Fix It!
1 vocabulary	2 prepositional phrases	? indents
	6 [main clauses]	? capitals
	6 subject-verb pairs (s v)	? commas
	3 openers	? end marks
		4 quotation marks
		3 apostrophes
		1 usage

Guessing confidently Frederick answered oh thats easy its The voyage Of The Dawn Treader, playing the game amused himself he chose another, Jennas **reputation** was only as good as her word

Rewrite It!

Week 18

Read It!   **Mark It!**   **Fix It!**   Day 4

1 vocabulary

2 prepositional phrases
4 [main clauses]
1 *who/which* clause (w/w)
1 *that* clause (that)
6 subject-verb pairs (s v)
4 openers

? indents
? capitals
? commas
? end marks
1 apostrophe

Dorinda who didnt know walked over to look, the words on the cover were One good turn deserves another reading the title made Dorinda **suspicious**, at that moment she decided, the game was over

Rewrite It! _____

108   Institute for Excellence in Writing *Fix It! Grammar: Frog Prince* Student Book Level 5

Learn It!

Who/Which Clause

You have learned that a **who/which clause** is a dependent clause that begins with the word *who* or *which* and follows the noun it describes.

The pronoun *who* has three forms: *who, whom, whose*.

> The pronoun **who** is a subjective case pronoun that functions as a subject.
> Use *who* when the subject of a *who* clause is *who*.
>
>   w/w   s   v
> Dorinda read to Frederick, (who listened eagerly).
>   The *who/which* clause describes *Frederick*, the noun it follows.
>   He listened eagerly.
>   The subject of the *who* clause is *who*.
>
> The pronoun **whom** is an objective case pronoun that functions as an object.
> Use *whom* when the subject of a *who* clause is not *who*.
>
>   w/w   s   v
> Dorinda read to Frederick, (whom she initially disliked).
>   The *who/which* clause describes *Frederick*, the noun it follows.
>   She initially disliked him.
>   The subject of the *who* clause is *she*. Begin the clause with *whom*.
>
> The pronoun **whose** is a possessive case pronoun that shows ownership.
> Use *whose* when the first word of either a *who* or a *which* clause functions as an adjective.
>
>   w/w   s   v
> Dorinda read to Frederick, (whose humor made her laugh).
>   The *who/which* clause describes *Frederick*, the noun it follows.
>   His humor made her laugh. Whose humor? *whose* (Frederick's)
>   The first word of the clause functions as an adjective. Begin the clause with *whose*.

Mark It!   Place parentheses around the *who/which* clause.
              Write **w/w** above the word *who, whom,* or *whose*.
              Write **v** above each verb and **s** above each subject.

Fix It!   Place a line through the incorrect pronoun and write the correct word above it.
              Use *who* when the subject of the *who* clause is *who*.
              Use *whom* when the subject of the *who* clause is not *who*.
              Use *whose* when the first word functions as an adjective.

Homophone

A **homophone** is a word that sounds like another word but is spelled differently and has a different meaning. Do not confuse *whose* with *who's*.

   Whose is a possessive pronoun that functions as an adjective.
   Who's is a contraction for *who is*. It includes both a subject (who) and a verb (is).
   You can use *who's* to begin a *who* clause only when the subject of the clause is *who*.

Who, Whom, or Whose?

Week 12 you learned that pronouns have 3 cases: subjective, objective, and possessive. Here is a portion of the chart on page 67.

3 Cases	Subjective	Objective	Possessive
Function (job)	subject predicate pronoun	direct object object of preposition	adjective
	he	him	his
	who	whom	whose

The pronoun *he* has three forms: *he, him, his*. Use *he* when the pronoun functions as a subject, *him* when the pronoun functions as an object, and *his* when the pronoun functions as an adjective in order to show ownership.

The pronoun *who* also has three forms: *who, whom, whose*. Use *who* when the pronoun functions as a subject, *whom* when the pronoun functions as an object, and *whose* when the pronoun functions as an adjective in order to show ownership.

Read each sentence. Should the dependent clause begin with *who, whom,* or *whose*? Write the correct word in the blank.

Dorinda, _____ situation was distressing, valued the library's distractions.

Frederick, _____ Dorinda accompanied, had a particular book in mind.

Frederick, _____ wanted to teach Dorinda, found the right book.

The main character, _____ name was Scarlett, fancied extravagant parties.

Dorinda admired Scarlett, _____ sunny personality won her many friends.

Scarlett, _____ Dorinda related to, planned a lavish party for her friends.

The friends _____ accepted the invitation admired the swan centerpiece.

Scarlett's puppy, _____ she spoiled, ate a cupcake.

Week 19

Day 1

Read It!

1 vocabulary

Mark It!

1 coordinating conjunction (cc)
2 prepositional phrases
3 [main clauses]
1 *who/which* clause (w/w)
4 subject-verb pairs (s v)
3 openers

Fix It!

? indents
? capitals
? commas
? end marks
1 usage

The frog who she detested had irritated her again she slammed the book down and **ignobly** fled to the palace grounds along the way she approached the well.

Rewrite It!

Week 19

Read It!	Mark It!	Fix It!	Day 2
1 vocabulary	1 <u>prepositional phrase</u> 2 [main clauses] 2 *who/which* clauses (w/w) 4 subject-verb pairs (s v) 2 openers	? indents ? capitals ? commas ? end marks 2 usage	

Suddenly she notices an old woman who's feeble hands were struggling to draw water from the deep well the woman **futilely** tried to turn the crank which would not budge.

Rewrite It! _____

_____

_____

_____

_____

112 Institute for Excellence in Writing *Fix It! Grammar: Frog Prince* Student Book Level 5

Read It!	Mark It!	Fix It!	Week 19
			Day 3
1 vocabulary	1 coordinating conjunction (cc)	? indents	
	1 prepositional phrase	? capitals	
	3 [main clauses]	? commas	
	1 *who/which* clause (w/w)	? end marks	
	4 subject-verb pairs (s v)	2 apostrophes	
	3 openers	1 usage	

Clearly her finger's ached **hampering** her task grasping the wooden bucket proved useless hearing steps the woman turned toward the girl who rude stared but didnt offer any assistance.

Rewrite It!

Week 19

Read It! | **Mark It!** | **Fix It!** | Day 4

1 vocabulary

1 coordinating conjunction (cc)
2 prepositional phrases
4 [main clauses]
4 subject-verb pairs (s v)

? indents
? capitals
? commas
? end marks
4 quotation marks
1 usage

Lovely princess the woman began I have arthritis in my hands and me cannot lift the **brimming** bucket would you kindly fetch me a cup of water

Rewrite It!

Learn It!

Overusing Coordinating Conjunctions

Week 2 you learned that a coordinating conjunction (cc) connects the same type of words, phrases, or clauses. The items must be grammatically the same: two or more adjectives, two or more prepositional phrases, two or more main clauses, and so forth.

> [Frederick ate fresh crickets], ~~and~~ burping loudly.
>> *And* incorrectly connects the noun *crickets* and the participial (-ing) phrase *burping loudly*. These items are not grammatically the same.

> ~~And~~ Dorinda laughed.
>> In formal writing a sentence should not start with a cc; in dialogue it may.

Fix It!   When a *cc* is used incorrectly, remove it or rewrite the sentence.

Week 10 you learned that one way to fix a run-on is to connect two main clauses with a comma + cc. **PATTERN MC, cc MC.**

Of the seven coordinating conjunctions, *and* is the most common and most overused. The pattern *MC, and MC* is effective when *and* is the most logical way to relate the two main clauses.

FANBOYS
for, and, nor, but, or, yet, so

Same Idea
The two clauses happen at the same time and express similar ideas.

> The chef made Frederick fly soup, and the maids fluffed his pillow.
>> Both sentences refer to the special treatment that Frederick enjoyed.

Sequential
The second clause happens after the first.

> The orderly brought Frederick fly soup, and he gratefully drank it.
>> Frederick drank the soup after the orderly brought it to him.

Writers can overuse the coordinating conjunction *and*. Check that *and* is the best way to connect the main clauses. If the main clauses express different ideas, they belong in separate sentences.

Fix It!   When the main clauses express different ideas, replace the *comma + and* with a period. Capitalize the first word of the new sentence.

> Because of its vast collection, [Frederick spent time in the library]**.** ~~and~~ [**h**e developed a guessing game with book titles].

Week 20
Day 1

Read It!	Mark It!	Fix It!
1 vocabulary	1 coordinating conjunction (cc)	? indents
	4 [main clauses]	? capitals
	1 *that* clause (that)	? commas
	5 subject-verb pairs (s v)	? end marks
	2 openers	2 quotation marks
		1 apostrophe
		1 usage

Tossing her golden locks Dorinda impulsively turned away why do people think I am his servant she grumbled. Treating other's attentively, and respectfully **evaded** her.

Rewrite It! _____

Week 20

Day 2

Read It!	Mark It!	Fix It!
1 vocabulary	2 coordinating conjunctions (cc)	? indents
	3 prepositional phrases	? capitals
	4 [main clauses]	? commas
	4 subject-verb pairs (s v)	? end marks
	1 invisible *who/which* clause (w/w)	1 semicolon
	3 openers	1 usage

Manners were essential, politeness was expected the old lady a fairy in disguise **brandished** her wand, and zapped princess Dorinda into a toad. And at last, the Princess would receive their punishment.

Rewrite It! _____

118   Institute for Excellence in Writing   *Fix It! Grammar: Frog Prince* Student Book Level 5

Week 20
Day 3

Read It!	Mark It!	Fix It!
1 vocabulary	2 coordinating conjunctions (cc)	? indents
	2 <u>prepositional phrases</u>	? capitals
	2 [main clauses]	? commas
	2 *who/which* clauses (w/w)	? end marks
	1 *that* clause (that)	1 usage
	5 subject-verb pairs (s v)	
	2 openers	

Instantly Dorinda plummeted to the ground, and all that remains was her crown which was miniaturized to fit her diminished stature and her beauty spot which was **prominent**, among the other toady warts.

Rewrite It!

Read It!	Mark It!	Fix It!	Week 20
1 vocabulary	1 coordinating conjunction (cc)	? indents	Day 4
	3 prepositional phrases	? capitals	
	4 [main clauses]	? commas	
	1 *who/which* clause (w/w)	? end marks	
	1 adverb clause (AC)	1 usage	
	6 subject-verb pairs (s v)		

That will teach you the fairy snapped, you must learn humility, as a toad, and if you find a noble **gallant** prince, who kiss you in kindheartedness you will be restored to normal

Rewrite It! _____

Learn It!

Run-On

Week 10 you learned that a **run-on** occurs when a sentence has main clauses that are not connected properly. A run-on can be either a **fused sentence** or a **comma splice**.

You also learned three simple ways to fix a run-on:
- Place a period at the end of each main clause.
- **;** Use a semicolon when two main clauses express a single idea and are similar in length or construction.
- **, cc** Use a comma + coordinating conjunction (cc) when a cc logically expresses the relationship between the two main clauses.

A fourth way to fix a run-on is to change one of the clauses into an adverb clause by inserting a www word. Use a comma after, not before, an adverb clause.

Adverb Clause

[Dorinda's reduced height was a problem], *because* [attendants were not used to looking down].

> This passage contains two main clauses connected with a comma, which is a run-on (comma splice). Fix the run-on by inserting a www word before the second main clause, forming a dependent adverb clause. **PATTERN MC AC**

If [The princess rested on the floor in the great hall], [someone might step on her].

> This passage contains two main clauses connected with no punctuation, which is a run-on (fused sentence). Fix the run-on by inserting a www word before the first main clause, forming a dependent clause. **PATTERN AC, MC**

Continue to look for and fix run-ons. Fix It! will indicate if you should fix a run-on with a coordinating conjunction (cc) or with an adverb clause (AC). Follow the comma rules.

Fix It   To *fix a run-on with cc*, insert a cc between two main clauses. Follow comma rule. **PATTERN MC, cc MC**

Dorinda deserved her punishment, *but* she did not like it.

> To *fix a run-on with AC*, insert a www word before a main clause, making it an adverb clause. Follow comma rules. **PATTERN AC, MC or MC AC**

Although Dorinda deserved her punishment, she did not like it.

Dorinda deserved her punishment *although* she did not like it.

Contrasting Items

A **contrast** shows a striking difference between things. In writing we often use the words *not*, *although*, *while*, or *whereas* to show contrast.

, Use a comma to separate contrasting parts of a sentence.

Use a comma to contrast, not compare.

Use a comma before *not* when it begins a contrasting phrase.

Everyone treated Dorinda as a toad**, not** a princess.
> A toad is strikingly different from a princess. Use a comma.

Use a comma before the www words *although*, *while*, or *whereas* when the adverb clause is strikingly different from the main clause before it.

You have learned you should not place a comma before an adverb clause (MC AC). Contrasting items, however, do take commas. Therefore, when an adverb clause is strikingly different from the main clause before it, use a comma. When two comma rules contradict, follow the rule that says to use a comma.

Palace staff used to cater to her**, whereas** now they mocked her.
> The adverb clause *whereas now they mocked her* is strikingly different from the statement *Palace staff used to cater to her*.

Fix It! Use a comma before *not* when it begins a contrasting phrase.
Use a comma before *although*, *while*, or *whereas* when it begins a contrasting clause.

Dorinda was rude, not gracious.

She loathed her transformation, although there was one real benefit.

She could hide in rooms and eavesdrop, while that was impossible before.

Read It!	Mark It!	Fix It!	Week 21
1 vocabulary	1 coordinating conjunction (cc)	? indents	Day 1
	4 prepositional phrases	? capitals	
	3 [main clauses]	? commas	
	1 *that* clause (that)	? end marks	
	4 subject-verb pairs (s v)	1 usage	
		(fix run-on with AC)	

Every day, the princess **mourned** her new lot in life. She found it difficult to convince anyone at the palace of her true identity, the crown, and beauty spot proved, she is the princess.

Rewrite It!

Read It!	Mark It!	Fix It!	Week 21
1 vocabulary	3 <u>prepositional phrases</u>	? indents	Day 2
	4 [main clauses]	? capitals	
	1 *who/which* clause (w/w)	? commas	
	1 adverb clause (AC)	? end marks	
	6 subject-verb pairs (s v)	4 quotation marks	
	1 opener	(fix run-on with cc)	

Lady Constance puzzled over the crown which looked familiar she tested Dorinda. If you truly are the princess she began Tell me about your **bona fide** wart not about that silly, beauty spot

Rewrite It! _____
_____
_____
_____
_____

Read It!	Mark It!	Fix It!	Week 21
			Day 3
1 vocabulary	2 <u>prepositional phrases</u>	? indents	
	6 [main clauses]	? capitals	
	1 *that* clause (that)	? commas	
	7 subject-verb pairs (s v)	? end marks	
	2 openers	4 quotation marks	
		2 apostrophes	
		1 number	

Luckily, that one was easy its true I have a wart, hiding behind all my hair Dorinda croaked, a palace maid **snickered** thats the reason she never let us style her hair in 2 braids

Rewrite It! _____

Week 21
Day 4

Read It!	Mark It!	Fix It!
1 vocabulary	1 coordinating conjunction (cc)	? indents
	5 [main clauses]	? capitals
	1 adverb clause (AC)	? commas
	6 subject-verb pairs (s v)	? end marks
		2 quotation marks
		1 apostrophe
		2 usage
		(fix run-on with AC)

Dorinda glared. Lady Constance wasnt convinced, she pressed her again what was your nickname, when you were a toddler. Dorinda sighs **testily**, and tries to roll her eyes.

Rewrite It!

Learn It!

Words as Words
When referring to a specific word as a word, italicize the word or place it in quotation marks. If handwriting, place the word in quotation marks.

> Dorinda used "please" to get her own way.
>
> Dorinda used [the word] "please" to get her own way.
>
> If you can insert "the word" before the word in question, it is a word used as a word.

Single Quotation Marks
Use **single quotation marks** for a quotation inside another quotation. The inside quotation may be the direct quote of someone's words, a title that needs quotations, or a word used as a word.

Fix It   Use quotations marks around words used as words.
           Add single quotation marks for a quotation inside another quotation.

> Dorinda's friends called her "Toady" because of the wart on her head.
>
> Frederick said, "My favorite poem is 'The Purple Cow.'"

Adjective Clause and Appositive Phrase
Week 15 you learned that an adjective can be a single word, a phrase, or a clause.
A **clause** is a group of related words that contains both a subject and a verb.
A **phrase** is a group of related words that contains either a noun or a verb, never both.

An **adjective clause** commonly begins with *who, whom, whose,* or *which* and includes a subject and a verb. An adjective clause can also begin with *when, where,* or *that.* The entire clause describes the noun it follows and does the job of an adjective.

> The toad (who wore a crown) was Princess Dorinda.
>
> *Who wore a crown* describes *toad*, the noun it follows. It begins with the word *who* and includes a subject (who) and a verb (wore).

An **appositive** is a noun or noun phrase that renames the noun it follows. It is a phrase because it includes a noun, never a verb.

> Princess Dorinda, the toad, felt sorry for herself.
>
> *The toad* is a noun phrase that renames the noun *Princess Dorinda*. It includes an article (the) and a noun (toad), not a verb.
>
> Another name for an appositive is the invisible *who/which* clause.
>
> Princess Dorinda, (who was) a toad, felt sorry for herself. Because the subject and verb (who was) are removed, the appositive is a phrase, not a clause.

Clause
subject + verb

Phrase
noun or verb, never both

Phrase or Clause?
A **phrase** is a group of related words that contains either a noun or a verb, never both.
A **clause** is a group of related words that contains both a subject and a verb.

Read each sentence and decide if the bolded words form a phrase or a clause.
  Circle the correct answer.

Lady Constance, **who raised the girls**, tested the toad's story.

    phrase   **clause**

Lady Constance, **their governess**, wondered if a toad could be Dorinda.

    phrase   **clause**

The toad's story, **which was an incredible tale**, seemed unbelievable.

    phrase   **clause**

Frederick, **a prince in disguise**, believed the toad.

    phrase   **clause**

Identify the opener as a #2 prepositional opener or a #5 clausal opener.
  Insert a comma if needed.

② prepositional

Pattern:
preposition + noun
(no verb)

comma if 5+ words

⑤ clausal

Pattern:
www word +
subject + verb

comma after clause
AC, MC

[ ] Since the fairy had changed Dorinda only Frederick believed her.

[ ] Since that horrible event Dorinda felt sad.

[ ] As she was no longer human Dorinda viewed the world differently.

[ ] As a toad Dorinda better appreciated Frederick.

[ ] Before her transformation Dorinda cared only about herself.

[ ] After the fairy changed her Dorinda was more sympathetic.

[ ] Until the event at the well Dorinda was thoroughly selfish.

[ ] Until she was restored Dorinda would learn to manage as a toad.

[ ] Because of Dorinda's new condition palace staff mocked her.

[ ] Because a toad's life was challenging Dorinda became grateful for any kindness.

Read It!	Mark It!	Fix It!	Week 22
			Day 1
1 vocabulary	4 prepositional phrases	? indents	
	4 [main clauses]	? capitals	
	1 *that* clause (that)	? commas	
	2 adverb clauses (AC)	? end marks	
	7 subject-verb pairs (s v)	4 quotation marks	
		1 apostrophe	
		(fix run-on with AC)	

as a child I was called toady I had a wart on the back of my head. As I aged my friends dropped it, since they realized that I wasnt a **toady** at all she snapped.

Rewrite It! _____

Week 22
Day 2

Read It!	**Mark It!**	**Fix It!**

1 vocabulary

1 coordinating conjunction (cc)
1 prepositional phrase
5 [main clauses]
1 *who/which* clause (w/w)
1 adverb clause (AC)
7 subject-verb pairs (s v)
4 openers

? indents
? capitals
? commas
? end marks
1 usage
(fix run-on with cc)

The palace took her in no one wanted to touch her. Her skin in fact were rough warty and **repulsive** some acknowledged her whereas others ignored her the footmen, who once pampered her, snubbed her.

Rewrite It!

Read It!	Mark It!	Fix It!	Week 22
1 vocabulary	1 coordinating conjunction (cc)	? indents	Day 3
	1 prepositional phrase	? capitals	
	2 [main clauses]	? commas	
	1 adverb clause (AC)	? end marks	
	3 subject-verb pairs (s v)		
	1 invisible *who/which* clause (w/w)		
	2 openers		

Maribella normally a sympathetic sister shuddered, whenever Dorinda **pattered**, into the room and even King Morton had nothing hopeful to offer his daughter.

Rewrite It!

Week 22
Day 4

Read It! | **Mark It!** | **Fix It!**

1 vocabulary

3 prepositional phrases
4 [main clauses]
4 subject-verb pairs (s v)

? indents
? capitals
? commas
? end marks
1 apostrophe
(fix run-on with AC)

Dorindas basic needs were met the **luster** had gone out of her life. Moping around the palace Dorinda complained constantly. Living as a toad devastated the princess

Rewrite It! _____

Learn It!

#4 -ing Opener
Week 5 you learned that a **#4 -ing opener** is a sentence that begins with a participial (-ing) phrase. A legal, grammatical #4 sentence opener follows the PATTERN **-ing word/phrase, main clause.**

Legal #4 Opener
A #4 -ing opener is a legal, grammatically correct #4 -ing opener when the thing after the comma (subject of main clause) is the thing doing the inging.

④ -ing
Adjusting his crown, King Morton sighed.

> *King Morton* is the thing (subject of main clause) after the comma. *King Morton* is doing the *adjusting*. This is a legal #4 -ing opener.

Illegal #4 Opener
A #4 -ing opener is an illegal, grammatically incorrect #4 -ing opener when the thing after the comma is not the thing doing the inging.

~~④~~ -ing
Adjusting his crown, it was heavy.

> *It* is the thing (subject of main clause) after the comma. *It* (the crown) is not doing the *adjusting*.
>
> This is an illegal #4 -ing opener and must be rewritten so that the person adjusting the crown is the thing (subject of main clause) after the comma.

~~④~~ -ing
Raising his voice, King Morton's impatience was obvious.

> It looks like King Morton is the thing after the comma. However, *King Morton's* is an adjective describing *impatience*. *Impatience* is not doing the *raising*.
>
> This is an illegal #4 -ing opener and must be rewritten so that King Morton, the person raising his voice, is the thing (subject of main clause) after the comma.

Find It! Check that the thing (subject of main clause) after the comma is the thing doing the inging.

Fix It! Rewrite if necessary.

④ -ing   *heavy*   **King Morton sighed.**
Adjusting his∧crown, ~~it was heavy~~.

④ -ing   **King Morton showed impatience.**
Raising his voice, ~~King Morton's impatience was obvious~~.

There is often more than one way to rewrite an illegal #4 sentence.

What Is the Sentence Opener?

As you learned Week 18, an impostor #4 begins with a #1 subject opener (the subject of the sentence) or a #2 prepositional opener (concerning, according to, regarding, during).

A legal #4 -ing opener follows the **PATTERN -ing word/phrase, main clause.**
The thing after the comma is the thing doing the inging.

An illegal #4 appears to follow the pattern, but the thing after the comma is not the thing doing the inging. The sentence is grammatically incorrect.

Read each sentence and decide if it begins with a #1 subject opener, #2 prepositional opener, #4 -ing participial opener or if the sentence is illegal (grammatically incorrect).
  Remove the comma if it is incorrect.

Dipping her bread in the fly soup, improved its taste.

  #1   #2   #4   illegal

Dripping in cream, Dorinda gobbled her bread.

  #1   #2   #4   illegal

During the afternoon, Frederick and Dorinda escaped to the library.

  #1   #2   #4   illegal

According to the head librarian, Frederick's book sat on the lowest shelf.

  #1   #2   #4   illegal

Hopping into the room, Frederick reached the bookshelf before Dorinda.

  #1   #2   #4   illegal

Leaping onto the footstool, Dorinda's back was sore.

  #1   #2   #4   illegal

Straining her back, made Dorinda irritable.

  #1   #2   #4   illegal

Opening the cover, Frederick sighed with contentment.

  #1   #2   #4   illegal

Read It!	Mark It!	Fix It!	Week 23
1 vocabulary	2 prepositional phrases	? indents	Day 1
	2 [main clauses]	? capitals	
	1 adverb clause (AC)	? commas	
	3 subject-verb pairs (s v)	? end marks	
	2 openers	1 illegal #4 opener	

Miserably, Dorinda wandered into the infirmary to **commiserate**, with her fellow amphibian. Mending rapidly Dorinda shared her gloomy thoughts, while Frederick listened sympathetically.

Rewrite It!

Week 23

Day 2

Read It!	Mark It!	Fix It!
1 vocabulary	1 coordinating conjunction (cc)	? indents
	1 prepositional phrase	? capitals
	3 [main clauses]	? commas
	1 who/which clause (w/w)	? end marks
	2 adverb clauses (AC)	2 quotation marks
	6 subject-verb pairs (s v)	2 apostrophes
	3 openers	1 usage

According to Frederick "being a frog wasnt that dreadful," while people werent always **humane** he was free to live as he pleased. Dorinda whom remained discouraged listened yet doubted.

Rewrite It! _____

Week 23

Day 3

Read It!	Mark It!	Fix It!
1 vocabulary	1 coordinating conjunction (cc)	? indents
	2 prepositional phrases	? capitals
	2 [main clauses]	? commas
	1 adverb clause (AC)	? end marks
	3 subject-verb pairs (s v)	2 quotation marks
	1 invisible *who/which* clause (w/w)	1 illegal #4 opener
	2 openers	

Trying to cheer her Dorinda agreed when Frederick offered to read a few stories he **regaled** her with humorous, fairy tales and wild stirring adventures, from the novel "the arabian nights."

Rewrite It!

Week 23

Read It!   **Mark It!**   **Fix It!**   Day 4

1 vocabulary

2 coordinating conjunctions (cc)
3 prepositional phrases
3 [main clauses]
3 subject-verb pairs (s v)
3 openers

? indents
? capitals
? commas
? end marks
1 apostrophe

Day after day Frederick entertained Dorinda. Gradually, she grew to appreciate his companionship, and to respect his positive **demeanor**, and living daily, without complaint characterized Fredericks life.

Rewrite It! _____

_____

_____

_____

138   Institute for Excellence in Writing   *Fix It! Grammar: Frog Prince* Student Book Level 5

Learn It!

Usage with Affect and Effect
Usage errors occur when a word is used incorrectly.

                        v
Dorinda was deeply affected by her transformation.
   Affect is a verb that means to have an influence or to cause.

         n
One effect of becoming a toad was surprisingly positive.
   Effect is a noun that means the result of some action.

Fix It!   Cross out the incorrect use of *affect* or *effect*.

Trials did not negatively affect/~~effect~~ Frederick.

Dorinda noticed the ~~affect~~/effect of his positive attitude.

Verb Review
Every verb has a subject. A verb acts alone or in phrases to perform different actions.
   An **action verb** (av) shows action or ownership.
   A **linking verb** (lv) links the subject to a noun or to an adjective.
   A **helping verb** (hv) helps an action verb or a linking verb. The helping verb and the verb it helps (action or linking) form a verb phrase.

Mark every subject. Mark every verb as an action verb (*av*), linking verb (*lv*), or helping verb (*hv*) in the following sentences.

Frederick thought that he would gag at the strange food.

He was surprised that he did not choke but swallowed it easily.

The food tasted bitter, but it satisfied his hunger.

The chef kindly prepared and served him insect delicacies.

Frederick had encouraged Dorinda to eat, but she refused.

She should have been grateful.

Review It!   Weeks 24–25 mark every verb as an action verb (*av*), linking verb (*lv*), or helping verb (*hv*).

Semicolon Review
A **semicolon** connects two main clauses that are closely related. The two main clauses express a single idea and are similar in length or construction.

Put a √ in the blanks of the following sentences that use a semicolon correctly.
Put an X in the blank of those that misuse the semicolon. Replace misused semicolons with periods.

____ Frederick counted ten flies in his soup; around the bowl and above the table hovered twenty more flies watching for the next dish.

____ The frog side of his personality enjoyed the flies; the human side was disgusted by them.

____ The orderly was kind to bring him fly soup on a tray; that way, spills were better contained.

____ Frederick sometimes savored a snail; he even relished an occasional slug.

____ Dorinda could not eat a spider; she would not touch the worm.

____ Frederick explained that mealworms and crickets were healthy food for toads; Dorinda shuddered at the mere thought of them.

Week 24
Day 1

Read It!	Mark It!	Fix It!
1 vocabulary	1 prepositional phrase	? indents
	2 [main clauses]	? capitals
	1 adverb clause (AC)	? commas
	3 subject-verb pairs (s v)	? end marks
	2 openers	1 apostrophe

Frederick always cheerfully greeted the orderly delivering his **odious** fly soup he didnt grumble, although the chef served him chocolate-covered beetles for dessert.

Rewrite It!

Week 24

Day 2

Read It!	Mark It!	Fix It!
1 vocabulary	2 coordinating conjunctions (cc)	? indents
	3 prepositional phrases	? capitals
	3 [main clauses]	? commas
	3 subject-verb pairs (s v)	? end marks
	2 openers	1 apostrophe
		2 usage
		1 illegal #4

Stumbling over his hurt leg Frederick didnt **chastise** Dorinda for her clumsiness, but readily forgave her, and she was grateful. His joyful attitude had a positive affect/effect on her.

Rewrite It! _____

_____

_____

_____

142   Institute for Excellence in Writing *Fix It! Grammar: Frog Prince* Student Book Level 5

Read It!	Mark It!	Fix It!	Week 24
1 vocabulary	2 prepositional phrases 5 [main clauses] 5 subject-verb pairs (s v)	? indents ? capitals ? commas ? end marks 4 quotation marks 1 number 1 usage (fix run-on with AC)	Day 3

How do you always remain so cheerful, Dorinda inquired 1 day. Unpleasant things happen you show **empathy** for others. Clearly trials do not affect/effect you

Rewrite It!

Week 24

Day 4

Read It!	Mark It!	Fix It!
1 vocabulary	1 coordinating conjunction (cc)	? indents
	2 prepositional phrases	? capitals
	5 [main clauses]	? commas
	2 adverb clauses (AC)	? end marks
	7 subject-verb pairs (s v)	2 quotation marks
		1 semicolon
		1 apostrophe

Oh thats simple. When I am angry folks avoid me, when I am kind they spend time with me. After all why should I be **discontent** I am comfortable fed and watered

Rewrite It! _____

_____

_____

_____

_____

144   Institute for Excellence in Writing *Fix It! Grammar: Frog Prince* Student Book Level 5

Learn It!

Usage with Between and Among
Usage errors occur when a word is used incorrectly.

Surely <u>between the two</u> of them, they could get along.
> *Between* is a preposition that refers to two items.

<u>Among their various activities</u> Dorinda enjoyed reading best.
> *Among* is a preposition that refers to three or more items.

Fix It!   Cross out the incorrect use of *among* or *between*.

Dorinda searched for berries among/~~between~~ the worms on her plate.

Frederick waited for Dorinda ~~among~~/between the twin pillars.

Comparative and Superlative Adjectives
Comparative and superlative adjectives describe a noun by making a comparison.

A **comparative adjective** compares two items. Form it by adding the adverbs *more* or *less* or the suffix *-er* to an adjective.

Dorinda was the younger daughter; Maribella was the older daughter.
> This sentence compares two girls: Dorinda and Maribella. The comparative adjectives *younger* and *older* are used.

Dorinda was younger than all of her cousins.
> One or both of the items may form a group. Although this sentence mentions all of her cousins, it compares two items: Dorinda and cousins. The comparative adjective *younger* is used.

Than signals a comparison of two items.

A **superlative adjective** compares three or more items. Form it by adding the adverbs *most* or *least* or the suffix *-est* to an adjective.

The great hall was the largest and most majestic room in the castle.
> This sentence compares the great hall with all the rooms in the castle. Since there are more than two rooms, the superlative adjectives *largest* and *most majestic* are used.

Follow these rules to form comparative and superlative adjectives.

Do not make a double comparison.
> Incorrect: She was *more younger* than her sister.

one syllable add suffix	three or more syllables use the adverbs	two syllables add suffix or use the adverbs	Some words form irregular comparatives and superlatives.	
-er -est	more or less most or least	In some cases, either way is acceptable although one form may be more common than the other.		
young younger youngest	**dangerous** more or less dangerous most or least dangerous	**clever** cleverer or more clever cleverest or most clever	**good** better best	**bad** worse worst

Fix It!   Cross out the incorrect comparative or superlative adjective.

Frederick was kinder/~~kindest~~ than Dorinda.

More on Quotation Marks

On Day 3 Frederick begins reading a story to Dorinda. Since he is speaking the words of the story, each paragraph must open with quotation marks to remind the reader that someone is still speaking. Closing quotation marks are used only when the speaker has finished.

Noun and Pronoun Function Review

A **noun** names a person, place, thing, or idea. A **pronoun** replaces a noun in order to avoid repetition. Week 11 you learned that both nouns and pronouns perform many functions (jobs) in a sentence; however, they can do only one function (job) at a time.

A **subject** is a noun or pronoun that performs a verb action. It tells who or what the clause is about.

An **object of the preposition** is a noun or pronoun at the end of a prepositional phrase.
PATTERN preposition + noun (no verb)

A **noun of direct address** is a noun used to directly address someone. It only appears in a quoted sentence.

A **direct object** is a noun or pronoun that follows an action verb and answers the question *what* or *whom*. A direct object receives the verb's action. That means it completes the verb's meaning.

A **predicate noun** is a noun or pronoun that follows a linking verb and answers the question *what* or *who*. A predicate noun renames the subject. The subject and predicate noun are different names for the same person, place, thing, or idea.

An **appositive** is a noun or noun phrase that renames the noun that comes immediately before it. It is a phrase because it includes a noun, never a verb.

In the following sentences mark every verb as an action verb (*av*), linking verb (*lv*), or helping verb (*hv*). Mark the function of every noun and pronoun.

Frederick asked, "Dorinda, can we play a game?"

Frederick and Dorinda played a game.

They played checkers, a game on the table.

Cribbage was another game on the table.

Review It!   Continue to mark every verb as *av*, *lv*, or *hv*.

This week mark every subject noun (*sn*), subject pronoun (*sp*), object of the preposition (*op*), noun of direct address (*nda*), direct object (*do*), predicate noun (*pn*), and appositive (*app*).

Read It!	Mark It!	Fix It!	Week 25
1 vocabulary	13 noun/pronoun jobs	? indents	Day 1
	6 prepositional phrases	? capitals	
	3 [main clauses]	? commas	
	1 *that* clause (that)	? end marks	
	1 adverb clause (AC)	1 semicolon	
	5 subject-verb pairs (s v)	1 usage	
	3 openers		

The next day, Frederick **rummaged** through the bookshelves in the library, he remembered a tale that his mother had read to him, when he was a boy; he searched for the story among/between the books.

Rewrite It!

Week 25

Day 2

Read It!	Mark It!	Fix It!
1 vocabulary	13 noun/pronoun jobs	? indent
	1 conjunction (cc)	? capitals
	2 prepositional phrases	? commas
	4 [main clauses]	? end marks
	1 adverb clause (AC)	1 semicolon
	5 subject-verb pairs (s v)	2 quotation marks
	3 openers	1 number
		1 usage

At last he saw a thin book among/between 2 large volumes. He desired this **precise** book, because it included the hound and the king's nephew. She would hear the story, she would learn a lesson.

Rewrite It! _____

_____

_____

_____

148   Institute for Excellence in Writing *Fix It! Grammar: Frog Prince* Student Book Level 5

Week 25
Day 3

Read It! **Mark It!** **Fix It!**

Mark the openers in the story that Frederick reads.
Do not mark openers for dialogue or conversational quotations between characters.

1 vocabulary	11 noun/pronoun jobs	? indents
	2 prepositional phrases	? capitals
	5 [main clauses]	? commas
	1 adverb clause (AC)	? end marks
	6 subject-verb pairs (s v)	2 apostrophes
	1 invisible *who/which* clause (w/w)	1 number
	3 openers	1 usage

"Dorinda listen as I read. "King Arthur" he began "was riding with his nephew. Robert the elder/eldest son of his sisters 3 boys enjoyed the kings special favor regrettably he was a **mute** child.

Since Frederick has not finished reading the story, do not end the passage with quotation marks.

Rewrite It!

Week 25
Day 4

Read It!   **Mark It!**   **Fix It!**

1 vocabulary   9 noun/pronoun jobs   ? indents
                 3 prepositional phrases   ? capitals
                 4 [main clauses]   ? commas
                 5 subject-verb pairs (s v)   ? end marks
                 3 openers   1 apostrophe
                                                    1 usage
                                                    (fix run-on with cc)

They rode through the royal forest where they often hunted. Roberts beloved hound Balin remained, among/between them. They passed through a Cedar Grove Balin ran ahead barking **emphatically**.

Rewrite It!

Learn It!

Usage with Than and Then
Usage errors occur when a word is used incorrectly.

> The hound was brighter than its litter mates.
>> *Than* is a word used to show a comparison.
>> *Than* is often used with comparative adjectives.

> What happened then was unexpected.
>> *Then* is an adverb meaning next or immediately after.

Fix It!   Cross out the incorrect use of *than* or *then*.

> Robert ~~than~~/then knew something was wrong.

> More than/~~then~~ anything, he longed to alert his uncle.

Comparative Adjectives and Superlative Adjectives
Last week you learned the difference between comparative and superlative adjectives. In order to use the correct form of the adjective, determine how many items are being compared.

> Balin was the largest hound in the litter.
>> This sentence compares Balin with each individual hound in the litter, which would include three or more puppies.
>> The superlative adjective *largest* is used.

> Balin was larger than the other hounds in the litter.
>> Although this sentence mentions many hounds, the word *than* forms a comparison of two items. This sentence compares Balin with the litter (a group).
>> The comparative adjective *larger* is used.

Comparative and Superlative Adjective Review
Read each sentence and determine if it needs a comparative adjective or a superlative adjective.
   Fill in the blank with the comparative (add *more* or *-er*) or superlative (add *most* or *-est*) form of the adjective in parentheses.

Balin was the _____ hound in the litter of five pups. (clever)

He was trained to be the _____ runner of them all. (fast)

His eyesight was _____ than the eyesight of the other pups. (sharp)

He was _____ to danger than his master. (alert)

Read It!   **Mark It!**   **Fix It!**   Week 26
Day 1

1 vocabulary   2 <u>prepositional phrases</u>   ? indents
                4 [main clauses]   ? capitals
                1 adverb clause (AC)   ? commas
                5 subject-verb pairs (s v)   ? end marks
                3 openers   1 semicolon
                                                  2 usage
                                                  (fix run-on with cc)

Balin barked louder/loudest than/then ever before; Robert was surprised, since his hound never barked, without a **credible** reason. He recognized the sound as a warning, concern gripped his heart.

Rewrite It! _____

Week 26

Day 2

Read It!	Mark It!	Fix It!
1 vocabulary	1 coordinating conjunction (cc)	? indents
	3 prepositional phrases	? capitals
	2 [main clauses]	? commas
	1 who/which clause (w/w)	? end marks
	3 subject-verb pairs (s v)	
	2 openers	

By contrast his uncle seemed **undaunted**, or perhaps oblivious to the noise, which the dog was making riding for hours the king had developed a potent thirst.

Rewrite It!

Week 26
Day 3

Read It!	Mark It!	Fix It!
1 vocabulary	1 coordinating conjunction (cc)	? indents
	4 prepositional phrases	? capitals
	3 [main clauses]	? commas
	4 subject-verb pairs (s v)	? end marks
	3 openers	1 illegal #4
		1 usage

This paragraph correctly opens with quotation marks to remind the reader that someone is still speaking.

"At a mountain stream where cool water trickled over some rocks King Arthur knelt, and than/then cupped his hands it was a **mere** dribble. Longing for a drink the king's hands waited to fill with water.

Rewrite It!

Week 26

Day 4

Read It!	Mark It!	Fix It!
1 vocabulary	1 coordinating conjunction (cc)	? indents
	1 prepositional phrase	? capitals
	2 [main clauses]	? commas
	1 *that* clause (that)	? end marks
	2 adverb clauses (AC)	1 apostrophe
	5 subject-verb pairs (s v)	
	2 openers	

"Anxiously Robert watched, and listened, while Balin barked madly although he feared that something in the water might be **noxious** Robert couldnt warn his Uncle.

Rewrite It!

Review It!

Week 27

Commas with Cordinating Conjunctions

ACRONYM FANBOYS

Coordinating conjunctions connect the same type of words, phrases, or clauses.

, | a, b, and c
  | MC, cc MC

✗ | a and b
  | MC cc 2nd verb

Read the following sentences and underline the words, phrases, or clauses that each cc connects. Insert commas where needed.

The king was thirsty and eager to drink the water.

Balin grew anxious barked loudly and tried to warn the king.

Balin sensed something was wrong but Robert could not call out a warning.

Robert realized that something was wrong but could not call out a warning.

Robert knew that Balin was warning them and the water could be tainted.

Robert wiggled the king's hands and the water spilled.

Dialogue Review
Dialogue includes quoted sentences and attributions.

What is an attribution? _____

_____

What is the difference between a direct quote and an indirect quote?

_____

_____

Capitalization and punctuation mistakes in quotations are common. Read the following passage and fix the errors.

The king cried. "Stay where you are".

Robert longed to explain that, "he did not trust the water". If he could speak, he would say "the hound is warning you".

"Be quiet. The king commanded Balin we will leave only after I drink some water".

Week 27
Day 1

Read It!

1 vocabulary

Mark It!

1 coordinating conjunction (cc)
2 prepositional phrases
4 [main clauses]
1 *that* clause (that)
5 subject-verb pairs (s v)
3 openers

Fix It!

? indents
? capitals
? commas
? end marks
1 semicolon
1 apostrophe
(fix run-on with cc)

Robert knew that he should not interrupt the king, he had to find a way to alert him; thinking quickly Robert rushed to his uncles side, and knocked the water, from his hands. This **agitated** the king.

Rewrite It!

Week 27
Day 2

Read It!	Mark It!	Fix It!
1 vocabulary	1 coordinating conjunction (cc)	? indents
	1 prepositional phrase	? capitals
	6 [main clauses]	? commas
	6 subject-verb pairs (s v)	? end marks
	1 opener	4 quotation marks
		1 usage

"King Arthur shouted, I am **parched**, and need water." "He just wanted a drink Dorinda interrupted Robert should have trusted his uncle not his dog. Of course his uncle was wiser/wisest"

Rewrite It! _____

_____

_____

_____

_____

160 Institute for Excellence in Writing *Fix It! Grammar: Frog Prince* Student Book Level 5

Read It!	Mark It!	Fix It!	Week 27
1 vocabulary	2 prepositional phrases	? indents	Day 3
	3 [main clauses]	? capitals	
	1 *who/which* clause (w/w)	? commas	
	1 adverb clause (AC)	? end marks	
	5 subject-verb pairs (s v)	3 quotation marks	
		1 apostrophe	

Humans can be foolish stubborn creatures whereas animal's instinctively sense danger, which humans cannot **detect** Frederick commented listen to the rest of the story

No closing quotation mark because quote continues.

Rewrite It! _____

_____
_____
_____

Week 27

Read It!	Mark It!	Fix It!	Day 4
1 vocabulary	2 <u>prepositional phrases</u>	? indents	
	2 [main clauses]	? capitals	
	1 *that* clause (that)	? commas	
	1 adverb clause (AC)	? end marks	
	4 subject-verb pairs (s v)	1 apostrophe	
	2 openers	1 usage	

This paragraph correctly opens with quotation marks to remind the reader that someone is still speaking.

"Cupping his hands again King Arthur collected more of the precious liquid flowing over the rocks persistently Robert than/then **jiggled** his uncles' hands signaling that they should check the source, before they drank.

Rewrite It!

162   Institute for Excellence in Writing *Fix It! Grammar: Frog Prince* Student Book Level 5

Week 28

Review It!

Unnecessary Commas
Using the list below, explain why the comma is wrong.

A	subject + verb	I	#3 opener modifies verb
B	a and b	J	MC AC
C	MC cc 2nd verb	K	end-sentence participial (-ing)
D	comma splice	L	essential appositive
E	before prep phrase	M	essential adj clause begins with *who* or *which*
F	*that* clause		
G	cumulative adjectives	N	essential adj clause begins with *when* or *where*
H	#2 opener < 5 words		

__J__ Dorinda softened, as she listened to the story about King Arthur.

____ She wondered if she would be impatient, or if she would listen to the warning.

____ She realized, that like the king she had been unkind.

____ She was ashamed because she had mistreated the girls, seeking her friendship.

____ Dorinda once pushed her friend, Clarissa, off a swing.

____ In the same week, Dorinda made fun of Jane's haircut.

____ Clarissa forgave her, Jane did not.

____ Even Maribella suffered from Dorinda's early, childish behavior.

____ Knowingly, Dorinda faked tears when Maribella was praised.

____ Each birthday in Dorinda's youth, was more extravagant than the one before.

____ Dorinda pouted, and even cried if Maribella received a nicer gift.

____ She felt she was the one, who deserved the best!

____ She then thought of the garden, where she had met Frederick.

____ She realized much had changed, since that time.

Institute for Excellence in Writing *Fix It! Grammar: Frog Prince* Student Book Level 5   163

Read It!	Mark It!	Fix It!	
			Week 28
			Day 1
1 vocabulary	1 coordinating conjunction (cc)	? indents	
	1 prepositional phrase	? capitals	
	2 [main clauses]	? commas	
	1 who/which clause (w/w)	? end marks	
	3 subject-verb pairs (s v)	1 usage	
	2 openers		

The king who's frustration had escalated **callously** pushed Robert away, suddenly Balin appeared jumping on the king knocking him over and spilling the water.

Rewrite It!

| | **Read It!** | **Mark It!** | **Fix It!** | Week 28 |
| | | | | Day 2 |

Read It!
1 vocabulary

Mark It!
1 coordinating conjunction (cc)
4 prepositional phrases
3 [main clauses]
3 subject-verb pairs (s v)
1 opener

Fix It!
? indents
? capitals
? commas
? end marks
2 quotation marks

"King Arthur lost all patience because of your relentless **insubordination** you, and your miserable hound dog are forever banished from my Kingdom he snapped at his nephew cowering, at his uncle's rage.

Rewrite It! _____
_____
_____
_____
_____

Week 28
Day 3

Read It!	Mark It!	Fix It!
1 vocabulary	1 coordinating conjunction (cc)	? indents
	1 <u>prepositional phrase</u>	? capitals
	2 [main clauses]	? commas
	2 *that* clauses (that)	? end marks
	1 adverb clause (AC)	1 usage
	5 subject-verb pairs (s v)	
	2 openers	

"**Grievingly** Robert turned away realizing, that he could insist on his way, or obey his uncle since he feared the king he decided that obedience was a better/best option.

Rewrite It!

Week 28 — Day 4

Read It!	Mark It!	Fix It!
1 vocabulary	4 prepositional phrases	? indents
	2 [main clauses]	? capitals
	3 subject-verb pairs (s v)	? commas
	2 openers	? end marks
		1 usage

"King Arthur decided to follow the path among/between the rocks to the top of the cliff where the water originated, wanting to drink without interference he made the **laborious** climb.

Rewrite It! _____

Week 29

Learn It!

Usage with Accept and Except
Usage errors occur when a word is used incorrectly.

Dorinda decided she would accept his offer of friendship.
> *Accept* is a verb meaning to take something offered or to agree to a suggestion.

Dorinda liked every dish the chef prepared except for caviar.
> *Except* is a preposition or conjunction that introduces the one person or thing that is not included in the main statement.

Fix It! Cross out the incorrect use of *accept* or *except*.

The chef worked everyday of the week ~~accept~~/except Sunday.

Frederick would gratefully accept/~~except~~ any dish they brought.

Sentence Opener Review
You have learned six types of sentence openers—six ways to open or begin a sentence. Using different sentence openers makes writing more interesting.

A #1 subject opener is written below. Use the idea of that sentence to write sentences that begin with each type of opener. Add commas where required. There are multiple right answers.

#1 Subject _____ *Dorinda no longer minded being a toad.* _____

#2 Prepositional _____

#3 -ly Adverb _____

#4 -ing _____

#5 Clausal _____

#6 Vss _____

Institute for Excellence in Writing *Fix It! Grammar: Frog Prince* Student Book Level 5   169

Week 29

Day 1

Read It!	Mark It!	Fix It!
1 vocabulary	1 coordinating conjunction (cc)	? indents
	1 prepositional phrase	? capitals
	4 [main clauses]	? commas
	4 subject-verb pairs (s v)	? end marks
	3 openers	1 apostrophe
		2 usage
		(fix run-on with cc)

"At the top, he discovered a dead snake. The enormous snakes poison had contaminated the water. Balin, and Robert had been trying too save the king's life, he had been two **arrogant** to listen.

Rewrite It! _____

Week 29
Day 2

Read It!	Mark It!	Fix It!
1 vocabulary	1 coordinating conjunction (cc)	? indents
	4 <u>prepositional phrases</u>	? capitals
	4 [main clauses]	? commas
	1 adverb clause (AC)	? end marks
	5 subject-verb pairs (s v)	2 quotation marks
	2 openers	1 usage

"When the king returned to the castle he called, for his nephew finding Robert in his room, with his servant Arthur humbled himself **contritely**. Can you accept/except my apology, and forgive me, He began.

Rewrite It! _____

_____

_____

_____

_____

Week 29
Day 3

Read It!	Mark It!	Fix It!
1 vocabulary	1 coordinating conjunction (cc)	? indents
	7 prepositional phrases	? capitals
	3 [main clauses]	? commas
	1 adverb clause (AC)	? end marks
	4 subject-verb pairs (s v)	2 quotation marks
		2 usage

While you trusted Balin myself depended on no one, accept/except myself. Robert for your loyalty I shall elevate you to the **coveted** position of arm bearer to the king and Balin shall dine on steak every day.

Rewrite It!

Week 29
Day 4

Read It!	Mark It!	Fix It!
1 vocabulary	1 coordinating conjunction (cc)	? indents
	4 prepositional phrases	? capitals
	4 [main clauses]	? commas
	2 *who/which* clauses (w/w)	? end marks
	6 subject-verb pairs (s v)	2 quotation marks
	1 opener	

"Robert signed to his servant who translated for him. Your safety matters I am pleased to serve you and I shall diligently work in the position which you are **entrusting** to me."

Rewrite It! _____

174   Institute for Excellence in Writing *Fix It! Grammar: Frog Prince* Student Book Level 5

Review It!

Fill in the blanks below with different parts of speech in order to create a silly story about Dorinda and Frederick.

After you have completed the list on this page, transfer your words to the blanks in the story on page 181.

1 noun _____

1 interjection _____

1 speaking verb _____

2 adjectives _____ _____

1 speaking verb _____

1 adjective _____

1 verb (past tense) _____

1 adjective _____

1 noun (clothing) _____

1 verb (past tense) _____

1 noun (body part) _____

1 -ly adverb _____

2 verbs (past tense) _____ _____

1 adjective _____

1 noun (food) _____

1 verb (past tense) _____

1 noun (body part) _____

2 -ing words _____ _____

1 verb (past tense) _____

1 interjection _____

1 adjective _____

1 speaking verb _____

1 -ly adverb _____

Read It!	**Mark It!**	**Fix It!**	Week 30
			Day 1

1 vocabulary

1 coordinating conjunction (cc)
2 prepositional phrases
3 [main clauses]
1 *who/which* clause (w/w)
4 subject-verb pairs (s v)
3 openers

? indents
? capitals
? commas
? end marks
1 apostrophe

At that moment, Dorinda realized the message of the story, she understood the offense, which was committed yet **poignantly** forgiven considering the boys kindness she examined her own heart.

Rewrite It! _____

Week 30
Day 2

Read It!	Mark It!	Fix It!
1 vocabulary	3 [main clauses]	? indents
	2 *that* clauses (that)	? capitals
	1 adverb clause (AC)	? commas
	6 subject-verb pairs (s v)	? end marks
	2 openers	

Why had she not recognized that her behavior had been **abhorrent**. Frederick had only desired that she keep her promise, truthfully she had treated him as dreadfully, as the king had treated Robert his nephew.

Rewrite It! _____

Week 30
Day 3

Read It!

1 vocabulary

Mark It!

3 prepositional phrases
2 [main clauses]
1 *that* clause (that)
3 subject-verb pairs (s v)
2 openers

Fix It!

? indents
? capitals
? commas
? end marks
1 apostrophe
2 usage

Dorinda now knew, that kindness to others was more/most beneficial than/then nurturing ones selfish interests, with heartfelt **remorse**, she kissed Frederick, on his cheek.

Rewrite It!

Week 30
Day 4

Read It! | **Mark It!** | **Fix It!**
1 vocabulary | 3 <u>prepositional phrases</u> | ? indents
 | 4 [main clauses] | ? capitals
 | 1 *that* clause (that) | ? commas
 | 5 subject-verb pairs (s v) | ? end marks
 | 3 openers | 1 apostrophe

What do you think Frederick did after that kiss.

He kissed her back of course poof the curses' were **reversed**, instantly, a noble gallant prince appeared beside a humble kindhearted princess.

Rewrite It! _____
_____
_____
_____
_____

Learn It!

Week 30

Use the words you chose on page 175 to complete the story.

Birthday Surprise

by _____

One _____ Princess Dorinda and Prince Frederick found a kitten.
              noun

"_____! Where did you come from?" Dorinda _____ .
    interjection   *speaking verb*

"Are you _____?"
        adjective

"He will be the _____ gift for Maribella's birthday!" Frederick
                  adjective

_____ .
speaking verb

Dorinda hid the kitten in her _____ bedroom. Later, Maribella
                                    adjective

_____ into the room, looking for a _____ _____ .
verb (past tense)   *adjective*   *noun (clothing)*

Out _____ the kitten, landing on Maribella's _____ . Maribella
    verb (past tense)   *noun (body part)*

_____ _____ from the room. She _____ right
-ly adverb   *verb (past tense)*   *verb (past tense)*

into Frederick, who was carrying a _____ birthday _____ . It
                                    adjective   *noun (food)*

flew up in the air and _____ on Maribella's _____ . She sat on
                      verb (past tense)   *noun (body part)*

the floor _____ . The kitten perched _____ on the stairs while
      -ing word   *-ing word*

Dorinda _____ Maribella.
    verb (past tense)

"_____! What a _____ birthday surprise!" Frederick
  interjection   *adjective*

_____ _____ .
speaking verb   *-ly adverb*

Appendices

Appendix I: Complete Story
    Frog Prince 185
Appendix II: Collection Pages
    -ly Adverb 195
    Strong Verb 197
    Quality Adjective 199
Appendix III: Lists
    Pronoun 201
    Preposition, Verb, Conjunction 202
    Clause 203
    Phrase 204
    Sentence Opener 205

Appendix I: Complete Story

Frog Prince

In the recent past in an obscure kingdom among the Alps, a decorous king reigned faithfully. His family line of monarchs stretched back to the Middle Ages. King Morton had inherited the throne from his father nearly three decades before. Like his father King Morton ruled fairly and showed compassion to all. As a kindhearted ruler, King Morton loved his subjects. The people of the land esteemed him. Maribella and Dorinda, the king's daughters, lived with him. Everyone in the land admired his devotion to his girls. His younger daughter, however, frustrated him greatly.

Princess Dorinda had been an obstinate child from toddlerhood. As a child she often escaped from the nursery and found mischief. She once stole into the throne room, swung on the chandeliers, and landed at the feet of the scandalized courtiers. On another occasion she upset the prestigious new chef and her staff. They were experimenting with sturgeon roe ice cream. Dorinda sneaked a taste and expected a sweet treat, but instead of bits of chocolate, the taste of salty fish eggs first surprised and then repulsed her.

The princess, who had earned a reputation for beauty, considered herself quite chic because she wore her hair in a French twist and had a beauty spot on her cheek. Her beauty was flawed by her reputation for fastidiousness and self-centeredness.

King Morton hoped that she would consider several young suitors. Dorinda refused them time after time, yet they continued to court her. None were wealthy, handsome, or titled enough for her highness. King Morton, whose patience was dwindling, shook his head in despair and sighed deeply when his daughter voiced her desires.

Clearly, Dorinda annoyed many in the palace. Lady Constance, who had cared for her since childhood, had virtually stopped training her young charge. Although Dorinda had seemed a lovable, tractable, and contented child in her youth, many years of indulgence had spoiled her. She complained constantly. Unfortunately, no expense had been spared to gratify the two girls when the girls' mother was alive. They enjoyed custom dolls with complete wardrobes and assorted furniture, but they always asked for more. When they were young girls, they were disappointed that their fairy-tale playground did not resemble Cinderella's castle. As a teenager Dorinda stomped her foot and pouted when a new television was delivered. Declaring it minuscule, she demanded a theater room with sound, lighting, and comfort. Although Lady Constance did not approve, she met Dorinda's demands because she did not want to argue with her.

On a crisp spring morning, Princess Dorinda played with her latest plaything, which was a golden ball. Tossing it up, she wandered among the plants in the conservatory.

From a distance the king observed his daughter and her golden ball. Eyeing the glass windows, he suggested, "Dorinda, why don't you toss that ball in the garden?"

Dorinda rolled her eyes. Crossly she grabbed her stylish boots and jacket and went outside. With her ball in hand, the princess roamed through the expansive castle gardens. Meandering aimlessly through the stately imperial gardens, Princess Dorinda repeatedly tossed her ball up and down and caught it with slick confidence. At the corner of the well, a most regrettable event occurred. Carelessly she tossed her precious golden ball too high, and down it fell with a splash. Dorinda gasped. The heavy ball sank to the bottom of the deep, dark well. Angry salty tears flowed, and Dorinda, who was inconsolable, stomped her foot in frustration.

"I've lost my golden baaall!" Dorinda wailed. "I would reward my benefactor handsomely if only I could have my ball back."

"I would be honored to assist you," a throaty voice offered.

Instantly Dorinda's tears dried as she looked around for the person who was speaking. In fact, she could turn her tears on and off on a whim. Seeing no one, Dorinda asked, "Oh! Who has proposed such a generous, thoughtful offer?"

Hopping toward her on the rim of the well, an amphibian croaked, "It was I."

As she let loose a spine-tingling shriek, Dorinda started to run. Of course, her inquisitiveness got the better of her, and she turned back to the frog. "How can you talk, Mr. Frog?"

"It's a long, dull story, but I might tell it to you in the future. Would you like me to find your ball?"

"Yes, I would appreciate that."

"I'll gladly do it with one unique stipulation," the frog responded.

"I'll do anything that you want! My dad will kill me if I lose that ball, which cost him a royal fortune," she replied. "You must jump in and retrieve my ball sitting at the bottom of the well."

"I'll salvage your ball if you'll allow me to stay for one night in the palace, feasting at your fancy table and eating from your own plate."

"Well, of course," Dorinda responded hastily.

The frog hopped into the water, disappeared for a few moments, and returned, holding Dorinda's treasure. Gleefully Dorinda snatched the wet, slippery ball.

"It's solid gold," he finally wheezed. Skipping back to the palace, Princess Dorinda didn't hear him pattering behind her. The exhausted amphibian hoped that Princess Dorinda's word was trustworthy.

While the royal family dined sumptuously, they heard a faint tap at the castle door. Within moments a footman appeared and delivered a message to Princess Dorinda.

"Princess," he began, "you have a visitor at the door."

Excusing herself from the table, Dorinda hastened away. She hoped that the visitor was her new friend, for she was eager to eat dessert with her.

When she opened the door, blood drained from her face. There sat the frog squatting and looking at Dorinda with sad huge eyes.

"You forgot your pledge to treat me hospitably," he croaked.

Dorinda slammed the door. Truthfully, she hoped that the audacious, annoying amphibian would leave, forget her promise, and never return.

"Dorinda, who knocked?" King Morton inquired when she returned.

Despite her deficiencies Dorinda truthfully answered her father. "It was a frog."

King Morton's eyes widened, and he inquired, "What did he want?"

Crying yet again, Dorinda sobbed the story of the frog's considerate rescue and of her foolish promise. She miserably wailed, "I will not touch that ugly, despicable thing!"

Dorinda's theatrics frustrated her father; her tears annoyed him. "Daughter," he urged, "you are a royal princess. Your word must be trustworthy."

Reluctantly Princess Dorinda slunk to the door. She opened it just wide enough for the frog to squeeze through. "You may enter," she sighed audibly.

Hopping behind her, the frog followed Dorinda to the elaborate dining hall. "I appreciate your hospitality, Sire. I'm Frederick," the frog volunteered.

"Dorinda, pick up Frederick," her father commanded, "and feed him from your golden plate."

"Yuck! Then I won't touch another bite," she whined.

Patiently King Morton, who valued integrity, explained that a promise was a promise. Additionally, he reminded Dorinda about her royal duties and the expectations of the people, the nation's citizens.

Dorinda complied. Because she would not touch the frog with her own precious fingers, she held her napkin between her thumb and first finger. Unceremoniously she grabbed one of Frederick's hind legs and deposited him on the table beside her plate. He was a revolting green amphibian. Promptly she receded into her chair.

After supper King Morton invited Frederick to the guest room, which was a splendid suite. Velvet carpeted the floor; silk blanketed the bed. Frederick knew that he would relish his palace stay.

Evidently, Dorinda, Maribella, and King Morton had not deduced the frog's true identity. Frederick was not a lowly frog but a royal prince. When he had lived at his father's castle, Frederick had been a swollen-headed, pretentious teenager.

On a humid afternoon in July, young Frederick had been riding his horse, a strong thoroughbred, through a forest in his father's vast kingdom. After he had ridden for several miles, his horse reared up because a thin young boy stood in the path.

"Please, sir, I've lost my way," the boy explained. "Can I have a ride out of this daunting forest?"

"Get out of my way, peasant," the rude, thoughtless prince retorted. He was oblivious that the boy was a wizard in disguise.

Instantly the boy's voice thundered, "For your lack of compassion and decency, you must spend your days as a frog, a worthless creature." Staring reproachfully, the boy zapped the air, and the prince found himself hopping off the saddle and plummeting to the ground. The wizard continued, "As a frog you might learn humility and gratitude for simple kindnesses which people offer you. You will be restored to normal if a princess kisses you in true kindheartedness. If you ever confess that you are a prince, you will be fated to froghood forever."

The frog had kept his secret for six long years, hoping he would eventually return to normal. Frederick had resided as a frog in King Morton's sequestered expansive garden, and he had wished one of the princesses, who frequently spent time in the garden, would be his friend. Unfortunately for him, he had met Dorinda before he had met Maribella.

That evening he assessed the situation and conjectured how to charm Dorinda, the younger princess.

The next morning during a substantial breakfast of omelets, pastries, and fruit, King Morton, who always treated his guests with generosity, graciously insisted that Frederick stay for a week.

Dorinda groaned. Glancing down, she noticed that Frederick's hind leg was inadvertently touching her omelet. "Ew!" she cried as she swept him from her plate and spitefully hurled him against the wall.

"Ow!" he grunted. "I believe my leg is broken!"

Dorinda feigned remorse for her unkind actions, mumbling an apology. "I wish I had broken all of your legs," she muttered pitilessly.

Dorinda's behavior mortified her father. King Morton gently lifted the frog, placed him on a silver tray, and carried him to the doctor caring for the animals. He ordered Dorinda to follow.

In the infirmary the palace vet positioned the frog on the adjustable exam table, where he treated his smallest patients. After he examined Frederick, he set the broken frog leg, which dangled oddly.

"Frogs are animals which heal slowly, so it will be a lengthy convalescence," the vet informed King Morton and Dorinda. "He will stay in the infirmary for a month."

Hearing the doctor's announcement, Dorinda became sullen. After her father insisted that she deliver Frederick's meals, she regretted the day when the accident happened. Dorinda resolved to avoid the infirmary, where Frederick now stayed. When the king ordered her to assist Frederick while he recuperated, she knew it would be difficult. She knew that she would have to treat him royally, but she could be a royal pain.

"Dorinda, read to Frederick your favorite stories in the imperial library," the king announced and walked away.

Every day Dorinda took Frederick to the library. Whenever they entered, the frog marveled at the hundreds of colorful books that covered the walls from floor to ceiling.

At last Frederick had an idea. "Let's play a game!" he eagerly proffered as he searched the row in front of him. "I'll read the first line of a story, and you tell me the name of the book." Agreeing hesitantly, Dorinda sat beside Frederick, whose scrawny skeletal fingers opened a book. "In the light of the moon a little egg lay on a leaf," read Frederick.

Dorinda thought for a moment. "That has to be *The Very Hungry Caterpillar*," she responded. She had enjoyed that book, a favorite of hers, since she was a young child.

Playing the game improved her mood. "Let me do one," she said. "There was a boy called Eustace Clarence Scrubb, and he almost deserved it." Hoping to stump Frederick, she smirked.

Guessing confidently, Frederick answered, "Oh! That's easy! It's *The Voyage of the Dawn Treader*!" Playing the game amused him. He chose another. "Jenna's reputation was only as good as her word."

Dorinda, who didn't know, walked over to look. The words on the cover were *One Good Turn Deserves Another*. Reading the title made Dorinda suspicious. At that moment she decided the game was over. The frog, whom she detested, had irritated her again. She slammed the book down and ignobly fled to the palace grounds. Along the way she approached the well.

Suddenly she noticed an old woman, whose feeble hands were struggling to draw water from the deep well. The woman futilely tried to turn the crank, which would not budge. Clearly, her fingers ached, hampering her task. Grasping the wooden bucket proved useless. Hearing steps, the woman turned toward the girl, who rudely stared but didn't offer any assistance.

"Lovely Princess," the woman began, "I have arthritis in my hands, and I cannot lift the brimming bucket. Would you kindly fetch me a cup of water?"

Tossing her golden locks, Dorinda impulsively turned away. "Why do people think I am their servant?" she grumbled. Treating others attentively and respectfully evaded her.

Manners were essential; politeness was expected. The old lady, a fairy in disguise, brandished her wand and zapped Princess Dorinda into a toad. At last the princess would receive her punishment. Instantly Dorinda plummeted to the ground. All that remained was her crown, which was miniaturized to fit her diminished stature, and her beauty spot, which was prominent among the other toady warts.

"That will teach you," the fairy snapped. "You must learn humility as a toad. If you find a noble, gallant prince who kisses you in kindheartedness, you will be restored to normal."

Every day the princess mourned her new lot in life. Although she found it difficult to convince anyone at the palace of her true identity, the crown and beauty spot proved she was the princess.

Lady Constance puzzled over the crown, which looked familiar, so she tested Dorinda. "If you truly are the princess," she began, "tell me about your bona fide wart, not about that silly beauty spot."

Luckily, that one was easy. "It's true. I have wart hiding behind all my hair," Dorinda croaked.

A palace maid snickered. "That's the reason she never let us style her hair in two braids."

Dorinda glared.

Because Lady Constance wasn't convinced, she pressed her again. "What was your nickname when you were a toddler?"

Appendix I: Complete Story

Dorinda sighed testily and tried to roll her eyes. "As a child I was called 'Toady' because I had a wart on the back of my head. As I aged, they dropped it since they realized that I wasn't a toady at all," she snapped.

The palace took her in, but no one wanted to touch her. Her skin, in fact, was rough, warty, and repulsive. Some acknowledged her, whereas others ignored her. The footmen, who once pampered her, snubbed her. Maribella, normally a sympathetic sister, shuddered whenever Dorinda pattered into the room. Even King Morton had nothing hopeful to offer his daughter. Although Dorinda's basic needs were met, the luster had gone out of her life. Moping around the palace, Dorinda complained constantly. Living as a toad devastated the princess.

Miserably Dorinda wandered into the infirmary to commiserate with her fellow amphibian. Mending rapidly, Frederick listened sympathetically while Dorinda shared her gloomy thoughts. According to Frederick being a frog wasn't that dreadful. While people weren't always humane, he was free to live as he pleased. Dorinda, who remained discouraged, listened yet doubted.

Trying to cheer her, Frederick offered to read a few stories. He regaled her with humorous fairy tales and wild, stirring adventures from the novel *The Arabian Nights*. Day after day, Frederick entertained Dorinda. Gradually she grew to appreciate his companionship and to respect his positive demeanor. Living daily without complaint characterized Frederick's life. Frederick always cheerfully greeted the orderly delivering his odious fly soup. He didn't grumble although the chef served him chocolate-covered beetles for dessert. Stumbling over his hurt leg, Dorinda was grateful that Frederick didn't chastise her for her clumsiness but readily forgave her. His joyful attitude had a positive effect on her.

"How do you always remain so cheerful?" Dorinda inquired one day. "Although unpleasant things happen, you show empathy for others. Clearly, trials do not affect you."

"Oh, that's simple. When I am angry, folks avoid me; when I am kind, they spend time with me. After all, why should I be discontent? I am comfortable, fed, and watered."

The next day Frederick rummaged through the bookshelves in the library. He remembered a tale that his mother had read to him when he was a boy. He searched for the story among the books. At last he saw a thin book between two large volumes. He desired this precise book because it included "The Hound and the King's Nephew." She would hear the story; she would learn a lesson.

"Dorinda, listen as I read.

"King Arthur," he began, "was riding with his nephew. Robert, the eldest son of his sister's three boys, enjoyed the king's special favor. Regrettably, he was a mute child. They rode through the royal forest, where they often hunted. Robert's beloved hound, Balin, remained between them. They passed through a cedar grove, and Balin ran ahead, barking emphatically. Balin barked louder than ever before. Robert was surprised since his hound never barked without a credible reason. He recognized the sound as a warning, and concern gripped his heart. By contrast, his uncle seemed undaunted or perhaps oblivious to the noise which the dog was making. Riding for hours, the king had developed a potent thirst.

"At a mountain stream, where cool water trickled over some rocks, King Arthur knelt and then cupped his hands. It was a mere dribble. Longing for a drink, the king waited for his hands to fill with water.

"Anxiously Robert watched and listened while Balin barked madly. Although he feared that something in the water might be noxious, Robert couldn't warn his uncle. Robert knew that he should not interrupt the king, but he had to find a way to alert him. Thinking quickly, Robert rushed to his uncle's side and knocked the water from his hands. This agitated the king.

"King Arthur shouted, 'I am parched and need water.'"

"He just wanted a drink," Dorinda interrupted. "Robert should have trusted his uncle, not his dog. Of course, his uncle was wiser."

"Humans can be foolish, stubborn creatures, whereas animals instinctively sense danger which humans cannot detect," Frederick commented. "Listen to the rest of the story.

"Cupping his hands again, King Arthur collected more of the precious liquid flowing over the rocks. Persistently Robert then jiggled his uncle's hands, signaling that they should check the source before they drank. The king, whose frustration had escalated, callously pushed Robert away. Suddenly Balin appeared, jumping on the king, knocking him over, and spilling the water.

"King Arthur lost all patience. 'Because of your relentless insubordination, you and your miserable hound dog are forever banished from my kingdom!' he snapped at his nephew cowering at his uncle's rage.

"Grievingly Robert turned away, realizing that he could insist on his way or obey his uncle. Since he feared the king, he decided that obedience was a better option.

"King Arthur decided to follow the path among the rocks to the top of the cliff, where the water originated. Wanting to drink without interference, he made the laborious climb.

"At the top he discovered a dead snake. The enormous snake's poison had contaminated the water. Balin and Robert had been trying to save the king's life, but he had been too arrogant to listen.

"When the king returned to the castle, he called for his nephew. Finding Robert in his room with his servant, Arthur humbled himself contritely. 'Can you accept my apology and forgive me?' he began. 'While you trusted Balin, I depended on no one except myself. Robert, for your loyalty I shall elevate you to the coveted position of arm bearer to the king, and Balin shall dine on steak every day.'

"Robert signed to his servant, who translated for him. 'Your safety matters. I am pleased to serve you, and I shall diligently work in the position which you are entrusting to me.'"

At that moment Dorinda realized the message of the story. She understood the offense which was committed yet poignantly forgiven. Considering the boy's kindness, she examined her own heart. Why had she not recognized that her behavior had been abhorrent? Frederick had only desired that she keep her promise. Truthfully, she had treated him as dreadfully as the king had treated Robert, his nephew. Dorinda now knew that kindness to others was more beneficial than nurturing one's selfish interests. With heartfelt remorse she kissed Frederick on his cheek.

What do you think Frederick did after that kiss? He kissed her back, of course.

Poof! The curses were reversed. Instantly a noble, gallant prince appeared beside a humble, kindhearted princess.

-ly Adverb
An **-ly adverb** dresses up writing because it creates a strong image or feeling.

Strong Verb
A **strong verb** dresses up writing because it creates a strong image or feeling. A strong verb is an action verb, never a linking or helping verb.

Appendix II: Collection Pages

Quality Adjective
A **quality adjective** dresses up writing because it creates a strong image or feeling. A quality adjective is more specific than a weak adjective, which is overused, boring, or vague.

Pronoun

A **pronoun** replaces a noun in order to avoid repetition.

A **personal pronoun** takes the place of common and proper nouns. It should agree with its antecedent in number, person, and case.

A **reflexive pronoun** ends in -self or -selves and refers to the subject of the same sentence.

An **intensive pronoun** ends in -*self* or -*selves*, functions as an appositive, and intensifies the noun or pronoun it refers to. Intensive pronouns can be removed from the sentence.

2 numbers	3 persons	Case / Function (job)	Subjective / subject predicate pronoun	Objective / object of preposition direct object indirect object	Possessive / adjective	Possessive / pronoun	Reflexive/Intensive
singular	1st		I	me	my	mine	myself
singular	2nd		you	you	your	yours	yourself
singular	3rd		he, she, it	him, her, it	his, her, its	his, hers, its	himself, herself, itself
plural	1st		we	us	our	ours	ourselves
plural	2nd		you	you	your	yours	yourselves
plural	3rd		they	them	their	theirs	themselves

A **relative pronoun** begins a dependent *who/which* clause. The pronoun *who* has three forms: *who* (subjective), *whom* (objective), *whose* (possessive).

who, whom, whose, which, that

An **interrogative pronoun** is used to ask a question.

what, whatever, which, whichever, who, whoever, whom, whose

A **demonstrative pronoun** points to a particular person or thing. When a word on the demonstrative list is placed before a noun, it functions as an adjective, not a pronoun.

this, that, these, those

An **indefinite pronoun** is not definite. It does not refer to any particular person or thing. When a word on the indefinite list is placed before a noun, it functions as an adjective, not a pronoun.

Singular and Plural	Plural	Singular			
all	both		each	much	one
any	few	another	either	neither	other
more	many	anybody	everybody	nobody	somebody
most	others	anyone	everyone	no one	someone
none	own	anything	everything	nothing	something
some	several	anywhere	everywhere	nowhere	somewhere

Preposition

A **preposition** starts a phrase that shows the relationship between a noun or pronoun and another word in the sentence. **PATTERN** preposition + noun (no verb)

This is not an exhaustive list. When in doubt, consult a dictionary.

aboard	amid	beneath	down	into	opposite	throughout	up
about	among	beside	during	like	out	to	upon
above	around	besides	except	minus	outside	toward	with
according to	as	between	for	near	over	under	within
across	at	beyond	from	of	past	underneath	without
after	because of	by	in	off	regarding	unlike	
against	before	concerning	inside	on	since	until	
along	behind	despite	instead of	onto	through	unto	

Verb

A **verb** shows action, links the subject to another word, or helps another verb.

An **action verb** shows action or ownership.

A **linking verb** links the subject to a noun or adjective.
    am, is, are, was, were, be, being, been (be verbs)
    seem, become, appear, grow, remain, taste, sound, smell, feel, look (verbs dealing with the senses)

A **helping verb** helps an action verb or a linking verb.
    am, is, are, was, were, be, being, been (be verbs)
    have, has, had, do, does, did, may, might, must, can, will, shall, could, would, should

Conjunction

A **conjunction** connects words, phrases, or clauses.

An **coordinating conjunction** (cc) connects the same type of words, phrases, or clauses.
    FANBOYS   for, and, nor, but, or, yet, so

A **subordinating conjunction** (www word) connects an adverb clause to a main clause.
    www.asia.b   when, while, where, as, since, if although, because
                   before, after, until, unless, whenever, whereas, than

Clause

A **clause** is a group of related words that contains both a subject and a verb.

Label the subject-verb pairs to determine how many clauses are in each sentence. Focus on the word that begins the clause and on its placement in the sentence to determine if it is a main clause or a dependent clause. After you have identified each clause, follow the comma rules.

Main Clause

A **main clause** expresses a complete thought, so it can stand alone as a sentence.

[Dorinda's dress was expensive].
Every sentence must have a main clause.

[Dorinda's dress was expensive]**, and** [this frustrated her father].
When a coordinating conjunction best expresses the relationship between the two main clauses, connect the main clauses with a comma and a coordinating conjunction. **MC, cc MC.**

[The dress had tiny pearls]**;** [it had gold embroidery].
When the main clauses express a single idea and are similar in length or construction, connect the main clauses with a semicolon. Use a semicolon sparingly. **MC; MC.**

Dependent Clause

A **dependent clause** does not express a complete thought, so it cannot stand alone as a sentence.

Adjective Clause

An **adjective clause** describes the noun it follows.

A *who/which* clause is an adjective clause.

[Dorinda's dress**,** (which she purchased online)**,** was expensive].
begins with *who, whom, whose, which, when, where, that* (a relative pronoun)
❟ use commas unless essential

Noun Clause

All the words in a **noun clause** work together to do a noun job.

A *that* clause is usually a noun clause.

[It frustrated the king] (that Dorinda purchased the dress).
commonly begins with *that* (a relative pronoun)
✗ do not use commas

Adverb Clause

An **adverb clause** modifies a verb in the sentence.

(Although Dorinda did not need another dress)**,** [she purchased this one] (because it had real gold).
begins with a www word (a subordinating conjunction)
❟ use a comma after but not before **AC, MC   MC AC**

Phrase
A **phrase** is a group of related words that contains either a noun or a verb, never both.

④ -ing
Watching his daughter, [King Morton(S) was relaxing(V) in the conservatory(V), his favorite place]. [Dorinda(S) had(V) grown(V) restless], wandering among the flowers.

Prepositional Phrase

in the conservatory   among the flowers

> A **prepositional phrase** begins with a preposition and ends with a noun.
>
> It adds imagery or information to a sentence because the entire phrase functions as an adjective describing a noun or as an adverb modifying a verb or adjective.
>
> , if a prepositional phrase opener has 5 + words
> around a transition

Verb Phrase

was relaxing   had grown

> A **verb phrase** includes a main verb (action or linking) and its helping verbs.
>
> It tells what a subject does in a sentence. The helping verbs often indicate the tense.
>
> ✗

Participial (-ing) Phrase

watching his daughter   wandering among the flowers

> A **participial (-ing) phrase** begins with a verb form that ends in -ing and usually includes additional words like adverbs, nouns, infinitives, prepositional phrases, or dependent clauses.
>
> It describes a noun because the entire phrase functions as an adjective. This is why the thing (subject of main clause) after the comma must be the thing doing the inging.
>
> , mid-sentence use commas unless essential
> end-sentence use a comma when it describes a noun other than the word directly before it

Appositive Phrase

his favorite place

> An **appositive phrase** is an appositive and the words that describe it. An appositive is a noun that renames the noun it follows. The appositive and the noun it follows are different names for the same person, place, thing, or idea.
>
> Because the comma rules for the *who/which* clause and the appositive phrase are the same, mentally insert *who* or *which* and the *be* verb to determine if the appositive phrase requires commas. This is why the appositive phrase is referred to as an invisible *who/which* clause.
>
> , use commas unless essential

Sentence Opener

A **sentence opener** is a descriptive word, phrase, or clause that is added to the beginning of a sentence.

① subject

The tired governess wondered how to teach Dorinda.

  begins with the subject of the sentence (may include article or adjective)

② prepositional

Before the queen's unfortunate death, Constance served the queen.

  begins with a prepositional phrase

  PATTERN preposition + noun (no verb)

  , | if 5 + words or transition

③ -ly adverb

Clearly, Dorinda embarrassed Lady Constance.

  begins with an -ly adverb

  , | if adverb modifies sentence (It was ___ that ___.)

④ -ing

Talking out of turn, Dorinda ignored regal protocol.

  begins with a participial phrase

  PATTERN -ing word/phrase, main clause

  , | after phrase

⑤ clausal

When Dorinda disregarded regal protocol, Constance chided the girl.

  begins with a www word (subordinating conjunction)

  PATTERN www word + subject + verb

  , | after clause (AC, MC)

⑥ vss

Dorinda exhausted her.

  2–5 words

Sometimes it appears that more than one sentence opener begins a sentence. When this happens, place the comma after the last opener. Number the sentence opener based on the first word of the sentence.